PORTFOLIO

THE NEW RULES FOR INVESTING NOW

James P. O'Shaughnessy has long been recognized as one of America's leading financial experts and a pioneer in quantitative equity analysis. *Barron's* has called him a "world beater" and a "statistical guru." The author of the *New York Times* business bestsellers *How to Retire Rich* and *What Works on Wall Street,* he has been profiled and interviewed extensively in the media. He manages mutual funds and portfolios for individuals and institutions in New York and lives in Connecticut with his wife and three children.

The New Rules
for Investing Now

Smart Portfolios
for the Next Fifteen Years

James P. O'Shaughnessy

PORTFOLIO

Previously published as *Predicting the Markets of Tomorrow*

For my mother and father

PORTFOLIO
Published by the Penguin Group
Penguin Group (USA) Inc., 375 Hudson Street, New York, New York 10014, U.S.A. · Penguin Group
(Canada), 90 Eglinton Avenue East, Suite 700, Toronto, Ontario M4P 2Y3, Canada (a division of Pearson
Penguin Canada Inc.) · Penguin Books Ltd, 80 Strand, London WC2R 0RL, England · Penguin Ireland,
25 St Stephen's Green, Dublin 2, Ireland (a division of Penguin Books Ltd) · Penguin Group (Australia),
250 Camberwell Road, Camberwell, Victoria 3124, Australia (a division of Pearson Australia Group Pty Ltd)
Penguin Books India Pvt Ltd, 11 Community Centre, Panchsheel Park, New Delhi – 110 017, India ·
Penguin Group (NZ), 67 Apollo Drive, Mairangi Bay, Auckland 1311, New Zealand (a division of
Pearson New Zealand Ltd) · Penguin Books (South Africa) (Pty) Ltd, 24 Sturdee Avenue,
Rosebank, Johannesburg 2196, South Africa

Penguin Books Ltd, Registered Offices:
80 Strand, London WC2R 0RL, England

First published in the United States of America under the title *Predicting the Markets of Tomorrow*
by Portfolio, a member of Penguin Group (USA) Inc. 2006
This paperback edition published 2007

1   3   5   7   9   10   8   6   4   2

Author's Note
This book does not constitute investment advice from the author, his employer, or other information
providers. This book contains statements and statistics that have been obtained from sources believed to be
reliable, but neither the author nor the information providers can guarantee the accuracy, completeness, or
timeliness of any of the information in this book, including, but not limited to, information originating
with the author, licensed by the author from information providers, or gathered by the author from publicly
available sources. Neither the author nor the information providers make any representations about the
suitability of the information contained in this book, nor shall have any liability, contingent or otherwise,
for any decision made or action taken by the reader in reliance upon such information. This book contains
various forward-looking statements based on the author's projections, hypotheses, forecasts, estimates, beliefs, and prognosis about future events. All forward-looking statements contained herein reflect solely the
author's opinions about such future events and are subject to significant uncertainty. Actual events may dif-
fer materially from those described in such forward-looking statements.

Publisher's Note
This publication is designed to provide accurate and authoritative information in regard to the subject matter covered. It is sold with the understanding that the publisher is not engaged in rendering legal, account-
ing, or other professional services. If you require legal advice or other expert assistance, you should seek the
services of a competent professional.

ISBN 1-59184-108-9 (hc.)
ISBN 978-1-59184-148-7 (pbk.)
CIP data available

Printed in the United States of America
Set in Legacy Serif
Designed by Jaime Putorti

Preface

> I know of no way of judging of the future but by
> the past.
>
> —Patrick Henry

In March of 2000, the S&P 500 marked its highest twenty-year real rate of return in over one hundred years. U.S. intermediate- and long-term government bonds reached the same high-water mark a year and a half later in September 2001. On the way to this summit, investors created one of the largest bubbles in history for trendy, new-era stocks and lived by the mantra that *it was different this time*. Near the end of this one-hundred-year flood in financial markets, many respected advisors were strongly recommending that investors allocate the bulk of their assets to large capitalization growth and technology stocks. Enthusiastic investors bid profitless companies to unprecedented valuations on little more than the ever-present hope that it *really was* different this time! It was widely accepted that a new era had dawned on Wall Street, requiring investors to throw out the old valuation rules and start using new metrics to price stocks according to their "true" value.

Simultaneously, the shares of small- and mid-cap stocks, as well as large capitalization value stocks, lagged both the S&P 500 and large capitalization growth stocks by the widest margins seen in the last seventy-seven years. What virtually every investor of the era "knew" through their experience in the market was that only a handful of the right stocks—large-cap growth or technology issues, or for the more conservative, an index fund mirroring the S&P 500—would be the ticket to continued double-digit growth for the foreseeable future.

It's time for investors to be reeducated.

I believe that what investors have "learned" over the past twenty years has clouded their expectations about what returns they might expect over the *next* twenty years, particularly concerning what types of stocks and bonds will offer the highest returns. Investors in 2007 still pine for returns that average over 15 to 20 percent per year and are still ignorant of the fact that we are seven years into a new market cycle that will reward stocks that are much different from the winners of the '80s and '90s. Careful analysis of long-term data shows us that financial markets have reached such great heights on several occasions in the past century. Studying the markets of yesterday can help us understand the markets of tomorrow and give us the new rules for investing now.

I hope that this book will be a call to action for investors who don't want to be left behind, and to all investors who want to reap the highest returns that the market might offer in the coming two decades.

The stakes could hardly be higher. We are facing a triple threat to our investment health: the future of Social Security is cloudy, corporate pension plans are massively underfunded, and many baby boomers' failure to save for retirement has left them frantically scrambling to find a way to a secure retirement. And despite Americans' fascination with the stock market over the past few decades, most are still financially illiterate. An April 27, 2005, article in the *New York Times* reported on a survey showing that the typical American knows virtually nothing about the economy or about how the stock market works. The article notes that "about half of American adults did not know that if they kept their money at home, in cash, they were at greater risk of losing ground to inflation than if they invested elsewhere." What's more, the average American gives very little thought to what he or she will need for retirement. According to a survey by the Principal Financial Group Inc., just 42 percent of American workers have done calculations to figure out if they are saving enough for retirement.

In all three of my previous books I have sought to understand why certain stocks go up while others decline. In *What Works on Wall Street,* I found that Wall Street consistently and methodically rewards securities with certain attributes just as surely as it punishes those with others. But it was only by looking at very long periods of data—fifty-five years for *What Works on Wall Street*—that this proved to be true. If you look at very short periods of time, what you see is meaningless noise. One five-year period would show small stocks performing well, another would show large-cap growth stocks on fire, a third might recommend value. When looking at the fullness of time, however, you see that certain types of stocks perform vastly better than others—and that there was a good reason for their superior performance.

The great bubble at the end of the 1990s led me to question if we had seen similar conditions before. Was there anything that the markets of yesterday could teach us about the markets of today and tomorrow? The answers surprised me and are the subject of this book. I recently conducted a study of the returns on stocks and bonds going back to 1925. Using Roger Ibbotson's superb EnCorr Analyzer program, I looked at the returns of stocks of several different kinds of companies—larger and smaller, faster or slower growing, undervalued or overvalued. Much to my astonishment, I found a largely unnoticed pattern: there is overwhelming evidence that throughout the twentieth century, the equity markets have moved in cycles or trends that last for twenty years before reverting and giving rise to a new cycle that takes the markets—and investors—in new directions.

Intrigued by the results back to 1925, I was able to analyze U.S. stock returns all the way back to the late 1790s by using total return data featured in Roger Ibbotson's book *Investment Markets: Gaining the Performance Advantage*. I found that the patterns of the twentieth century were virtually duplicated in the nineteenth century, confirming that reversion to the long-term mean is one of the ironclad rules of financial markets.

My newest research shows that the middle of the year 2000 marked the end of a momentous twenty-year cycle. During this period, the market (and investors' attention) was dominated by stocks of larger, faster-growing companies—like those in the S&P 500 and large-cap growth indexes—and long-term bonds, while they reached their highest ever twenty-year rates of return. The cycle we are now entering will be characterized by a very different dynamic. My research indicates that kind of high-test performance is over for those types of stocks and bonds.

In today's cycle, the one begun in 2000, the best returns will likely come from the stocks of small-size companies, mid-size companies, large company *value* stocks, and shorter duration, intermediate-term bonds. Ironically, and despite the excellent returns of the last seven years, the small- and mid-cap stocks that I believe will perform the best are little known and relatively ignored by most of today's investors. If you look at the returns since 2000, you can see that they have already begun their ascent. How can I be so confident in my predictions? History tends to repeat itself, especially in the financial markets. The past *can* show us the way to the future, primarily because of the market's strong tendency to revert to its mean.

Seven years ago, small-capitalization stocks and large-cap value stocks began outperforming the S&P 500 and large-cap growth stocks and while they may face short-term reversals, I believe they will continue to do so for the next fifteen years. Historically, stocks of smaller companies beat the stocks of larger companies in almost all rolling twenty-year periods since the mid-1920s—*but they haven't for the last twenty years.* Historically, the stocks of value companies beat the stocks of growth companies—*but they haven't for the last twenty years.* Because of the power of mean reversion, I now believe they will continue the strong long-term performance they have enjoyed since the start of this new cycle in March of 2000.

Investors are always flip-flopping between exuberance and despondence—but both extremes are irrational. Markets function the same way, moving from the mean to the extreme and back again; from speculative peaks to humbling busts. Look at the S&P 500. Its long-term real rate of return over any twenty-year period is 7.3 percent. Whether it is soaring above or foundering below that mean, it always heads back toward that 7.3 percent average return. Eventually it gets there.

The same is true for *other* types of stocks. For small-cap stocks, the long-term real rate of return over any twenty-year period is 10.42 percent, and they always try to get back to *that* mean. The same is true for value and growth stocks. We are now seven years into a new twenty-year cycle, where in all likelihood the trends from the last twenty-year cycle will reverse themselves. Readers who avail themselves of this data can do *substantially better* with their investments than those who continue to base their assumptions on what happened over the last twenty years.

Here's a quick preview of what you'll learn from this book:

◆ If you are a typical investor, you are currently overinvested in large-capitalization growth stocks and underinvested in mid- and small-cap stocks.

◆ Indexing to the S&P 500 has had its day. While many investors grew wealthy on the ride, that fun is over. The S&P 500 index will likely return only 3 to 5 percent annually over the next twenty years.

◆ Small-cap stocks, which began a rally in 2000, will continue to do significantly better than large-cap stocks over the next ten to fifteen years.

◆ Large-cap value stocks will once again outperform large-cap growth stocks.

◆ For the most aggressive investors, 40 percent of your stock portfolio should be in small- and mid-cap stocks. Another 40 percent should be in large-cap value stocks. Only the remaining 20 percent should be invested in large-cap growth companies.

◆ The prospects for long-term bonds are grim. Over the next twenty years, investors will be far better served by shorter duration and inflation-protected bonds.

◆ These correlations have persisted over long periods of time, and reversion to the mean is likely to continue.

◆ Investors with the capacity to invest in alternative investments such as hedge funds should seriously consider doing so.

Acknowledgments

While this book is an extension of the research I conducted for *What Works on Wall Street*, I needed much longer-term data to carefully study the market's twenty-year cycles. For this I am extremely indebted to Roger Ibbotson, a professor of economics at Yale University and the founder and namesake of Ibbotson Associates, the firm that supplies the data through its Ibbotson EnCorr Analyzer program. I am also deeply indebted to him and his colleagues for the extended data of U.S. stock market returns and inflation back to 1791 found in his marvelous book *Investment Markets: Gaining the Performance Advantage* (MGraw-Hill, 1987) that are also used in this book.

Thanks to Steve Leuthold and his colleagues at the Leuthold Group in Minneapolis, who graciously allowed me to reprint their work here. Steve's company has conducted superb quantitative research on the stock market and its performance at various valuation levels.

I am also indebted to the numerous academics and researchers quoted in this book. Their important work made it much easier for me to detect these trends and explain why they are likely to persist. I find the quality and depth of research available tremendously encouraging.

I owe my greatest debt of gratitude to my wife, Melissa. She has edited all four of my books and her expert hand always improves my work. She is truly the coauthor of my work, and I am deeply grateful for her assistance. Of course, all errors and omissions are entirely my own.

Contents

1

The Perfect Storm

> To be ignorant of what happened before you
> were born is to remain always a child.
>
> —Cicero

January 1, 2000—a new millennium dawning and all was right with the world. The United States stood unchallenged astride the world, the last and only superpower. Communism was vanquished in the former USSR, the Berlin Wall reduced to rubble, communist and socialist systems around the world in retreat, replaced by liberal democratic capitalism. President Clinton announced the end of the era of large government, the United States was at peace and prosperous, the government's coffers overflowed with a surplus—and a horde of first-time investors viewed themselves as heirs to a glimmering world. The world they knew, the world they had known for the last twenty years, was one of unlimited possibilities.

The NASDAQ had increased tenfold in the last decade. New-era stocks—virtually all linked to technology or the Internet—doubled and then doubled again. Making money seemed as simple as just making the decision to invest; investors felt double-digit returns were practically their birthright. You couldn't lose. A swarm of new investors descended upon the stock market, eager to make their fortune overnight. The most renowned analysts of the time called for a continuation of the "goldilocks economy," with brief and mild recessions and a Federal Reserve that would manage the vast U.S. economy so that all landings would be soft. Even the most cantankerous market bears were letting down their guard and learning to love the bull market. To the Greek chorus on Wall Street, it truly was different this time.

Many investors had tried to watch patiently from the sidelines, waiting for a market pullback before joining the fray. The problem was, the market rarely did pull back, and when it did turned right around and quickly raced past the old highs. The last pullback had been in the third quarter of 1998, when a host of problems—including Russia's default on its sovereign debt, the Asian markets collapsing into crisis, and the meltdown of one of the country's largest hedge funds, Long-Term Capital Management—had briefly put the nation's equities on sale.

But since that brief buying opportunity, investors continued to push shares of profitless companies skyward. They based many of their decisions on what market analysts were saying on CNBC—or even more likely on what they had read about a stock's prospects on one of the countless new Internet chat boards devoted to investing. Valuing investments the old-fashioned way—by analyzing their books, profits, dividends, and prospects for earnings and dividend growth over the longer term—was relegated to the dust-bin of history.

In this new era of unbound confidence, such traditional analysis reeked of dusty libraries and outmoded techniques. In the new era, all you had to do to get rich was to be in the game. It really didn't matter what stocks you bought, provided they were in the hot and sexy new industries of the time: technology companies, Internet companies, or just about anything associated with growth. Indeed, to focus on any traditional concept of valuation was to limit oneself, since under the new paradigm, the spoils went to those with "first mover" advantage, regardless of cost. Investing in stocks with the best valuations was considered to be hopelessly out of fashion and a marker for suckers who just "didn't get it."

It's Different This Time

The new-era mantras were "if you build it, they will come" and "it's different this time." Initial public offerings (IPOs) were all the rage, with investors going to great lengths to be put on "friends and family" lists. Stock analysts were the new rock stars, their views sought out by an eager and gullible public looking for any advantage in the marketplace. All the old methods of valuing a stock were replaced by metrics such as eyeballs per million, page views, and projected revenue growth. It was a true stock market fever.

Fueling the fire was the sheer fact that the numbers didn't lie. Someone who had invested $10,000 at the start of 1995 would have seen his account bloated with profit five years later. A conservative investor who simply invested $10,000 in an S&P 500 index fund in 1995 found it worth over $33,000 at the beginning of 2000, a gain of over 233 percent. But, as many of the best-selling business books at the time pointed out, indexing to the S&P 500 was just the *start* of good investing, with more "savvy" investors piling into anything.com and specialty technology funds.

Indeed, someone who concentrated their investments in areas of technology, like software and semiconductor manufacturers, would have seen their $10,000 soar in value to between $82,213 and $86,269! That's what investments made in 1995 in the S&P 500 semiconductor equipment index and what the S&P 500 software industry index grew to at the beginning of 2000. Investors took these average annual returns of over 50 percent per year as their birthright and believed that the party would never end.

The Unstoppable Money Machine

Money was on everybody's mind. They talked about it, read about it, surfed the Internet for it, and vowed to max out their 401(k) contributions and start an IRA. Mutual funds were among the primary beneficiaries of this speculative fever. According to the Investment Company Institute's 2000 Factbook on mutual funds (available online from the ICI at www.ici.org/pdf/factbooks), equity mutual fund assets increased by $913 billion between 1995 and 1999, with total assets increasing over 218 percent from $2.16 trillion at the start of 1995 to $6.85 trillion by the end of 1999. According to the report, "net flows went to the funds benefiting from relatively large technology stock investments. In a sample of 1,633 domestic stock funds, for example, the 10 percent with the highest net new cash flows had about one-third of their assets in technology stocks; roughly double that of the 10 percent of the lowest net flows. Investor preference for funds with significant exposure to the technology sector similarly was reflected in net new cash flows by investment objective. For example, capital appreciation funds nearly doubled their net flow in 1999 to $160 billion from $83 billion in 1998. In contrast, the net flow to funds with a total return objective fell to $16 billion in 1999 from $67 billion in 1998."

Most of this money was coming from first-time investors. According to Investment Company Institute research, "an estimated 48.4 million, or 47.4 percent, of all U.S. households owned mutual funds at the end of 1999. The growth in fund ownership occurred primarily in two household groups, those with incomes under $50,000, and those with financial decision-makers under age 55. The number of individual investors owning mutual funds rose to 82.8 million in 1999, from 77.3 million in 1998." What's more, the number of households investing in mutual funds had nearly doubled from 1992, when the bull market was already ten years old.

Mutual funds weren't the only beneficiaries of this speculative mania, either: business-related books, magazines, TV programs, and Internet sites all saw their sales, ratings, and page views soar. Looking at *BusinessWeek* magazine's best-seller lists in the late 1990s, a central theme was clear: "you, too, can get rich quickly." Between 1997 and 2000, the stock market reigned supreme on the best-seller list. Titles like *Wall Street Money Machine* and *Stock Market Miracles,* both by Wade B. Cook, dominated the list, along with other titles such as *The Nine Steps to Financial Freedom* by Suze Orman, *The Roaring 2000s* by Harry S. Dent, Jr., and *The Electronic Day Trader* by Marc Friedfertig and George West. (I should also admit that one of my books, *How to Retire Rich,* was on the list.)

CNBC, the all business news cable station, went from obscurity to ubiquity in under five years. At the height of the boom, CNBC's daytime ratings surpassed those of CNN. No matter where in the United States you went, you were sure to find CNBC churning out the market news.

In late 1999 I gave a speech in a tiny suburb of Atlanta. A waiter in a local restaurant told me that he and his friends on staff recognized me because they watched CNBC all the time. Several of my employees, returning from a trip to rural Tennessee, told me that even the TV sets in the local McDonald's there were tuned to CNBC. People from every stratum of society were fascinated and transfixed by the stock market, and the analysts they saw touting stocks on CNBC became minor celebrities.

Business magazines like *BusinessWeek, Fortune, Forbes,* and *Money* saw their circulations soar along with the stock market. Despite many skeptical articles about the market's prospects, the underlying fascination remained. *Money,* in particular, was a relentless cheerleader on behalf of the average shareholder. And while many of the articles in the various magazines outlined sound investment advice, the underlying theme remained the same: over time, equity markets are the only place to make money.

All We Ever Knew

At the beginning of the year 2000, rising stock markets were all many of us had ever known. It was certainly all I had known in my investing lifetime. I got married on August 6, 1982. I was just twenty-two years old at the time and already fascinated with the stock market. I vividly recall reading about the huge market upswing while overseas on my honeymoon. By the time I turned forty in the year 2000, I could look back at my entire adult life and see that for the most part, equity markets only went up.

Yes, there was the stock market crash in October 1987, when the market fell a terrifying 23 percent in one day, but it quickly bounced back from that and went on to new highs. During my adult life, most market downturns had been brief and swiftly forgotten as the stock market inevitably resumed its path upward. My nearly twenty-five years of marriage—in which my wife and I raised three children, lived in five houses, started and sold a business, and wrote three books on investing—all transpired with figure 1-1 as a backdrop.

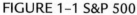

FIGURE 1–1 S&P 500

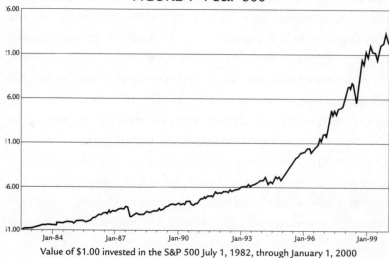

Value of $1.00 invested in the S&P 500 July 1, 1982, through January 1, 2000

The graph shows an almost uninterrupted ascent, with one dollar invested in the summer of 1982 growing to over $22 by the beginning of the year 2000. That's an extraordinary average annual compound return of 19.45 percent per year! An investor who opened a $10,000 tax-advantaged savings account in the summer of 1982 and invested it in the S&P 500 index would have seen his or her account grow to $224,205 at the beginning of 2000.

Every bit of experience over those seventeen years would lead us to conclude that the very best course is to stay invested in a simple index like the S&P 500 through thick and thin. The 1987 crash looks like a mere blip on the graph, as does every other downturn that occurred over the period. The Zeitgeist of the era was that growth trumped value, small-cap underperformed large-cap, and the simplest and best way to invest was to index your money to the S&P 500.

Born in 1960, and therefore part of one of the largest generations ever to begin investing in the stock market, I wasn't the only one getting this message. Thinking about retirement for the first time, millions of baby boomers looked back and saw only a rising tide in the stock market.

What's more, an investment in the S&P 500 was considered *conservative* for all but the most timid investors. In the late 1990s, the real action was in the large-cap growth and technology stocks that populate much of the NASDAQ index. At that time, many investors became enamored of an exchange traded fund that duplicated the returns of the NASDAQ index. Called the triple Q—after its ticker symbol—it compounded at an average annual rate of 46.88 percent between December 31, 1996, and December 31, 1999.

For many of the most aggressive investors, the only way to get *truly* rich was to trade individual stocks. A huge subculture emerged in the final years of the twentieth century: the day traders. For these investors, mostly neophytes overconfident in their stock-trading prowess, everything was about immediate gratification. At the height of the day trading boom, between September 1, 1998, and March 31, 2000, the returns of some of the day traders' favorite stocks went truly parabolic. During that period, RF Micro Devices Inc. rose from $1.80 to $67.20, a staggering increase of 3,575 percent! And it wasn't alone. EchoStar Communications Corp., Applied Micro Circuits, QUALCOMM, PMC-Sierra, JDS Uniphase, and CMGI all increased by more than 2,000 percent over the same period! These returns intoxicated a whole generation of investors, leading them to believe that the world had changed and we had finally reached a "new paradigm" where the old rules no longer applied and only those who rejected them would prosper. Polls at the time showed that investors expected to continue to earn double-digit returns on their stock portfolios over the next ten to fifteen years. What they didn't understand was that they were nearing the center of a perfect storm.

The Perfect Storm

J. M. Barker said, "Whenever you have a group of people thinking the same thing at the same time, you have one of the hardest emotional causes in the world to control." Was he ever right. At the end of 1999, trying to tell people that valuations in the stock market mattered was like trying to sell ice to Eskimos. Blinded to history by what they had experienced firsthand, most investors dismissed such sage and rational advice out of hand.

Like me, many had never experienced a bear market during their adult lives. As we will see later in the book, when it comes to shaping people's outlook regarding the stock market's future returns, personal experience almost always trumps centuries of historical data. People respond to vivid, immediate information. What they saw with their own eyes was a sizzling and awe-inspiring rise in stock prices. What they heard with their own ears was an entire chorus of analysts, stock bloggers, and traders telling them why it would never end. Much of this information appeals directly to the emotional rather than the rational part of the brain—and in that battle, the vivid story always trumps the boring facts.

The Wrong Lessons

At the end of 1999, almost no one knew that the previous twenty years were culminating into a nearly perfect storm in financial markets. Almost every "lesson" that investors had learned from those twenty years was wrong. Everyone *knew* that technology stocks were the only way to go; everyone *knew* that the stock market always turned around and quickly regained old highs; everyone *knew* that large-cap growth stocks outperformed small-cap stocks and value stocks; everyone *knew* that the only real risk was *not* being invested in these high-octane names. They also knew that stocks could trade at one hundred, two hundred, even three hundred times earnings, and never so much as back off a bit.

Long-term market history contradicted these "facts," however. For as long as we have data, in almost all twenty-year periods, high-priced growth stocks, like the technology stocks investors loved so much in the late 1990s, rarely outperformed value stocks or the broader market. What's more, during the twenty-year periods for which we have data, small stocks almost always outperformed large stocks. Thus, the twenty years ending on December 31, 1999, amounted to a perfect storm in financial markets. It was a time when stocks that usually perform well didn't, and when stocks that usually lag the market turned in eye-popping returns. These facts led many to challenge the new-era ideologues, warning of dire things to come when the bubble finally burst.

Contradicting this new-era paradigm was a risky proposition. Many investment professionals—myself included—who proclaimed that traditional valuations still mattered were ignored or dismissed. On April 22, 1999, I published the following, part of an article on my company's Web site, which I called the "Internet Contrarian":

> No other market mania has ever produced such outlandish valuations, and I believe that when the inevitable fall comes, it will be harder and faster than anything we've ever witnessed. . . . We are currently witnessing the biggest bubble the stock market has ever created. When the Internet insanity ends, truckloads of books will be turned out; endless comparisons to Dutch Tulip bulbs and Ponzi schemes will be made; and a whole generation of ex-day-traders will rue the day they were seduced by the siren song of the Internet. This mania is a creation of fantasy and ludicrous expectations and of the childlike notion that hope can prevail over experience. Legions of inexperienced people—many

of whom can't even begin to understand a balance sheet—believe that all they need do to secure their fortune is to plunk down their money on Anything.com and watch the profits roll in.

Near the top of any mania, you'll often see outright stupidity rewarded. The current myopia cannot and will not last. After every other market mania—*from tulip bulbs in 17th century Holland, to radio stocks in the 1920s, to aluminum stocks in the 50s, to computer stocks in the mid 1980s and the biotech craze of the early 1990s—those boring laws of economics* always *rear their very sane heads. Ultimately, a stock's price must be tied to the future cash payments a company will make to you as an owner. History shows us that the more you pay for each dollar of a company's revenue, the lower your total return. It does this because* it has to—*that's why economics is called "the dismal science."*

Because the numbers ultimately have to make sense, the majority of all currently public Internet companies are predestined to the ash heap of history. And even if we could see the future and identify the ultimate winner in e-commerce, at today's valuations it is probably already *over-priced. When people realize that the mania has dried up, and that "the greater fool" isn't there anymore, they'll all rush for the exits at the same time. And the same thing that drove Internet prices up—lack of liquidity married to irrational investors—will drive them down, only* more *quickly.*

It's Different This Time, *Really*

Immediately after I posted the article, e-mails mocking my naïveté came pouring in. Decorum prohibits me from quoting some of the more strident messages I received, but the general tenor was that I was hopelessly out of touch with the new stock market realities. With a near religious fervor, my readers told me that the new-economy Internet stocks simply could not be valued the same as the old-economy "bricks and mortar" stocks. Time and again, I was told why the valuation metrics that used to work no longer would. Several people went so far as to suggest that if I did not adjust my thinking, I would soon be out of a job. One writer even tried to use the academic efficient market theory to explain why current valuations had to be correct, citing the theory's precept that current stock prices reflect all known information and therefore accurately reflect stocks' value.

Professor Robert Shiller forecast the collapse of the bubble in his remarkably prescient 2000 book, *Irrational Exuberance*. In a May 22, 2000, *Barron's* article, Professor Shiller is quoted as saying: "the market is high because of the combined effect of indifferent thinking by millions of people, very few of whom feel the need to perform careful research on the long-term investment value of the aggregate stock market, and who are motivated substantially by their emotions, random attentions, and perceptions of conventional wisdom." The author of the article goes on to point out that "in Shiller's estimation, the most pernicious influence on today's investors is the efficient market theory. It holds that the price of stocks of the market as a whole is fairer and rational at any point in time, because those prices reflect the collective wisdom of legions of informed investors who coolly assess the latest information affecting company profit prospects and impound the data into prices."

Researchers have found that investors' outlook and behavior is consistent and predictable. The body of work that catalogs this behavior is called *behavioral finance*. In chapter 6, I'll take a close look at the latest behavioral finance research, as it can help all investors avoid the speed traps and pitfalls that the market often presents. Later in the book I'll also show how people's attitudes and beliefs affect their outlook for the market, and explain why it is so difficult for people to change their expectations about future market returns. The combination of history and human nature conspires to make us seriously misjudge the future. For now, keep in mind that during the market bubble the majority of investors simply refused to listen to arguments that contradicted their hopes and dreams for untold stock market wealth.

New Millennium, Grim New Reality

During the first few years of this new century, investors came to understand a grim new reality—markets *can* and *will* go down. The bear market of March 2000 to March 2003 was the worst since the early 1970s, and few were spared: All of the new-era stocks, so beloved by investors in the 1990s, were crushed. All of the stocks mentioned earlier that gained more than 2,000 percent in just over a year plunged by more than 90 percent! RF Micro Devices, up more than 3,500 percent during the bubble, dropped from $67.20 a share to $3.80, a loss of 98.5 percent. Applied Micro Circuits Corp., trading at $75 a share, on March 31, 2000, plunged to $2.50 per share, a drop of 96 percent. Stocks like these contributed to the NASDAQ's plunge of 80 percent from its high. The new-era stocks weren't the only casualties, either—the S&P 500 lost more than 47 percent on an inflation-adjusted basis.

For the first time in nearly twenty years, investors learned that it *wasn't* different this time, that valuation *does* matter, and that buying stocks on a whim and a hunch just because everyone else was doing it was the height of foolishness. Investors also noticed that not all stocks were crushed during the crash—in fact, some stocks actually went up during the period. Smaller-cap stocks with much lower valuations and large stocks with high dividends and low PE's offered significantly better returns than the large-cap S&P 500 and large-cap growth mutual funds.

The market bubble and its crushing aftermath led many investors to question their core beliefs about how to be a successful investor. With dreams of market riches in tatters and hopes for early retirement eliminated, investors began asking much harder questions. Had there been markets like this in the past? If so, what happened afterward? How does inflation affect my portfolio? What about taxes? When investors lose money, they start asking tougher, more critical questions. They get smarter, and they want answers. I'll now attempt to answer some of these questions and see what the past might teach us about the future.

Chapter One Highlights

- ◆ Investors drastically overweight their recent experiences in the market and are prone to create anchors for their expectations for the future from their recent past. Knowledge of this problem does not make it go away.

- ◆ There have been a number of "new-era" manias in which investors came to believe that their own time in history was truly unique and that only the explicit rejection of past valuation techniques would lead to successful investments. The three most recent periods were those ending in 1929, 1968, and 1999.

◆ Market bubbles have *always* ended in bear markets where stocks revert to historically relevant valuations.

◆ Investors consistently make the same mistakes, and evaluating and understanding them will give the long-term investor an edge to improve the expected rate of return on his or her portfolio.

2

Where You Start Determines Where You End Up

> Human beings, who are almost unique in having
> the ability to learn from the experience of others,
> are also remarkable for their apparent
> disinclination to do so.
>
> —Douglas Adams

During the bull market of the 1980s and 1990s, the most common advice financial professionals gave investors was to ignore the market's short-term gyrations and focus on the long-term. I am a passionate advocate of this viewpoint. Focusing on the day-to-day movements of the stock market is one of the worst things you can do as an investor. Drawing on my continued devotion to long-term analysis, this chapter will outline how a careful analysis of the past can help us forecast where the market is headed and therefore make more intelligent, well-informed decisions about our investments in the future.

The Holy Grail: A Long-Term Outlook

Nearly every study conducted of people's investment behavior comes to the same conclusion: the more frequently investors adjust their portfolios, the worse their performance. Terry Odean, a professor of finance at the University of California at Berkeley, found that the more frequently an investor reviewed the performance of his or her portfolio, the more likely they were to trade in and out of various positions. This trading was extremely destructive to performance, resulting in returns that significantly lagged the general indexes.

One study that quantified this underperformance was conducted by Dalbar Financial Services, a Boston-based consulting firm. Dalbar found that investors' *actual* returns were significantly lower than the published returns for indexes and mutual funds. According to Dalbar's 2005 report, *Quantitative Analysis of Investor Behavior,* the average equity investor earned over 9 percent *less* annually than the S&P 500 over the last twenty years! This huge chasm was attributed to investors' trying to time the market and thus failing to keep their money in stocks for the entire time period.

Taking the Long View

Cognizant of this sobering statistic, financial advisors use the graph featured in figure 2–1 in an attempt to get investors to focus on longer periods of time. This is one of the most famous graphs in the financial literature, generated using research conducted by Roger Ibbotson, a professor of finance at Yale University and the founder and chairman of Ibbotson Associates in Chicago. The graph shows the growth of one dollar invested in the S&P 500 on June 30, 1927, through December 31, 2004. (While the data for the S&P 500 go back to January 1, 1926, I use June 30, 1927, to make it consistent with other returns I'll illustrate later in the book.) Over the nearly seventy-eight years covered, one dollar grows to over $2,000.

By helping investors focus on very long periods of time, financial advisors were able to show that in the long run, equities were unequivocally the best performing asset class. Looking at the graph, even the horrific bear markets of the early 1930s, the early 1970s, and the early 2000s appear as minor blips in the market's inexorable march upward. For this reason, the graph is used in thousands of brokerage offices, financial planning establishments, and in many books and seminars in an effort to educate the general public about the benefits of long-term investments in the U.S. stock market. Ibbotson's research on the long-term efficacy of equity investing has been broadly validated. In his seminal book *Stocks for the Long Run,* Jeremy Siegel shows that between 1802 and 2001, equities have outperformed all other asset classes, doing so with a remarkable degree of stability.

The message sank in. Investors so internalized the data from figure 2-1 that it began to guide their future expectations for their equity portfolios' returns. Even after the 2000–2002 bear market, polls reveal that investors still expect to earn between 10 and 15 percent annually. Unfortunately, while it is safe to say that over the next *seventy-eight years* equity investors can expect to earn over 10 percent annually in their portfolios, the same cannot be said for shorter spans of time. When asked about the returns they anticipate, investors often base their expectations for the next five to fifteen years on a *seventy-eight-year average.* This is a classic misuse of that annualized 10.32 percent return, for it fails to recognize that all that time smoothed out a lot of very jagged edges.

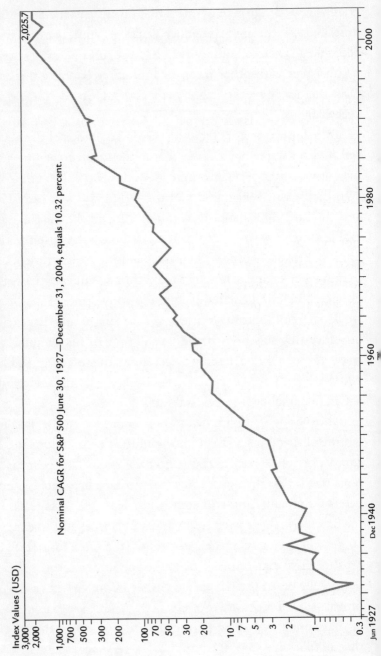

FIGURE 2–1 NOMINAL RETURN FOR S&P 500

Nominal CAGR for S&P 500 June 30, 1927–December 31, 2004, equals 10.32 percent.

Today's investors often use the seventy-eight-year average (which covers many market cycles) incorrectly, naïvely assuming that it is a good proxy for what to expect over the shorter term. By doing so, they blind themselves to a critical fact—the ups and downs and highs and lows of the market over all rolling fifteen- to twenty-year periods are dramatically more volatile than this very long-term 10 percent average would suggest.

On Average, I'm Fine

There's a wonderful joke about a fellow who has his head in a red hot oven and his feet in a bucket of ice, but nevertheless quips: "On average, I'm fine!" That's what investors are doing when they assume that the long-term annual average of 10.32 percent is applicable to their portfolio's returns over shorter periods of time. To get a realistic sense of what to expect, investors should look at the historical returns of equities and other investments that match their own expected holding periods. Say you, like me, are forty-five years old and want to retire when you're sixty-five. Rather than look at a seventy-eight-year average, you should look at the returns on various investments over *all* rolling twenty-year periods available to you. At my former firm, O'Shaughnessy Capital Management, we pioneered a technique utilizing rolling returns for all the investment strategies we offered. Using clients' personal time horizons, we could better inform them about the potential ups and downs of a particular strategy, and what their best, worst, and average expectations should be. We'll see shortly that such an analysis dramatically changes the range of returns you might anticipate from a variety of investments. Before doing so, however, we need to understand what types of returns we should be looking at in the first place.

Inflation: The Silent Return Killer

Another problem with the dramatic returns shown in figure 2–1 is that they are an illusion, because they fail to take the effects of inflation into account. The returns in figure 2–1 are absolutely accurate, but not terribly useful to investors. Why? Because they ignore the often pernicious and eroding effects of inflation. Inflation is sneaky—we don't pay nearly as much attention to it as we do to our investment returns, yet it invisibly robs us of purchasing power and thus of true return. You simply don't know how your investments have really performed until you've taken inflation into account.

Let's say you start out with a portfolio worth $10,000. Ten years later, it's worth $20,000 and your proud portfolio manager tells you that he's doubled your money. While your manager has indisputably doubled your money, you have no way of knowing whether he doubled your purchasing power—unless you look at inflation. Thus, if $10,000 bought you 100 units of your favorite goods and services ten years ago but those same 100 units now cost $20,000, your net increase in purchasing power is zero. That means your real return for the ten-year period is zero, even though your nominal return was 100 percent.

Studies have shown that investors consistently forget to make apples to apples comparisons by taking the effects of inflation into account. It's difficult for investors to consciously subtract the loss of purchasing power that inflation incurs. Many simply ignore it, making it difficult to make meaningful judgments.

Take real estate, for example. In 1963 the median price of a new house in the United States was $17,200. By 2004, the median price was $206,300. At first glance, it appears that new housing prices have skyrocketed over the past forty years, since the median-priced home in the United States now costs twelve times as much as it did in 1963. When you take inflation into account, and price the 1963 home in today's dollars, however, you see that the price of that 1963 house would be $108,016 in today's dollars—a more modest doubling in value over forty years.

The Importance of Being Real

Inflation lurks everywhere. Remember figure 1-1 in chapter 1, showing one dollar invested on June 30, 1982, growing to $21.94 by January of 2000? That was a nominal rate of return. When looking at the *real* rate of return, that dollar grew to just $12.62. Inflation distorts our ability to judge whether our investments have been truly successful or not. With very few exceptions, the stated returns for everything you might invest in—from mutual funds to real estate to individual stocks and bonds—are nominal rates of return, not real rates of return. In 1963 one dollar bought what $6.26 buys today. In 1927, one dollar bought what almost $11 buys today. This is vital to keep in mind, as the value of the dollar continues to decline over time.

By ignoring real rates of return, investors seriously misjudge which investments might offer the best returns. Let's take another look at real estate. The real rate of return on new U.S. homes was just 1.55 percent per year between 1963 and 2004. Over the same period, the S&P 500's real rate of return was 6.15 percent per year, and small-cap stocks compounded at over 10 percent per year! Thus, between 1963 and 2004 an investment in a U.S. home performed only slightly better than the 1.31 percent real rate of return offered by U.S. Treasury bills.

Comparing nominal and real rates of return can confuse stock and bond investors as well. During the 1970s, for example, many investors might have been content with their portfolios' performance: a $10,000 investment in the S&P 500 made in 1970 was worth $17,668 at the end of the decade, a nominal compound annual return of 5.86 percent. But after taking inflation into account, investors would have seen the truth—the 1970s were the worst decade for stocks in over one hundred years. The decade's real rate of return was a *loss* of 1.41 percent per year, reducing the real value of $10,000 to $8,676 by the end of 1979.

TABLE 2-1 NOMINAL AND REAL INFLATION-ADJUSTED RATES OF RETURN, JUNE 30, 1927–DECEMBER 31, 2004

Portfolio	$1 Becomes	Compound Average Annual Return
Nominal S&P 500	$2,025.70	10.32%
Real Inflation-Adjusted S&P 500	$187.30	6.98%
Nominal US Small Stocks	$11,448.40	12.82%
Real Inflation-Adjusted US Small Stocks	$1,058.40	9.40%
Nominal US Long-term Government Bonds	$58.32	5.39%
Real US Long-term Government Bonds	$5.39	2.20%
Nominal US 30 Day Treasury Bills	$17.03	3.73%
Real US 30 Day Treasury Bills	$1.57	0.59%

Source: Ibbotson EnCorr Analyzer

Table 2-1 shows the nominal versus real rates of return for stocks and bonds for the longer period between 1927 and 2004. Figure 2-2 shows both the nominal and real returns for the S&P

FIGURE 2-2 NOMINAL AND REAL RETURN FOR S&P 500

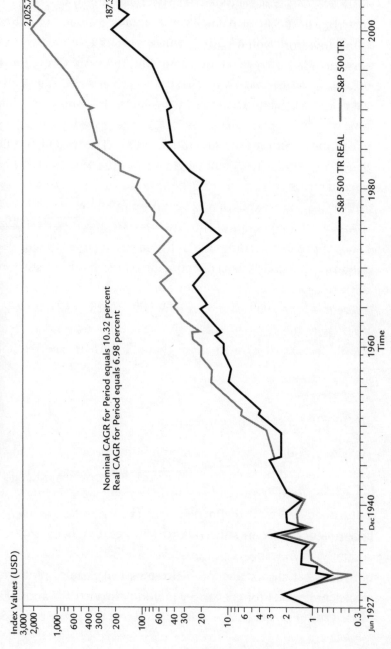

Nominal CAGR for Period equals 10.32 percent
Real CAGR for Period equals 6.98 percent

500 over the same period. The differences are so dramatic that from this point forward, I will consider only real rates of return.

Clearly, inflation-adjusted returns give us a much better idea about what to expect over long periods of time. After we adjust for inflation, we see that an investment in U.S. Treasury bills offers virtually no returns over long periods of time, turning one dollar invested nearly seventy-eight years ago into just $1.57 today! U.S. government bonds don't fare much better, growing a dollar into $5.39 over the same seventy-eight years. By comparing the real rates of return of Treasury bills, bonds, and stocks we see that, even after adjusting for inflation, stocks offer much higher rates of return. Over long periods of time the real rate of return to stocks is about 7 percent, turning one dollar invested seventy-eight years ago into $187 today. This is a good benchmark for investors, but for it to be a reasonable assumption, you would also need to have a seventy-eight-year time horizon for your portfolio! That's highly unlikely, and gets us to the key message of this chapter—investors should look at all rolling periods that match their expected holding period.

Rolling Twenty-Year Real Returns

As it turns out, there is a common holding period that many investors share. It is based on when people actually start saving and investing for their retirement—during middle age. During young adulthood—generally defined as ages twenty to thirty-nine—the majority of people are still net borrowers because they are starting a family, buying their first house, and so forth, and are therefore mostly consumers rather than investors. It isn't until their more prosperous middle years that people actually start to save and invest. Typically, this occurs in the mid-forties. If we assume that people are still planning to retire at age sixty-five, we see that the

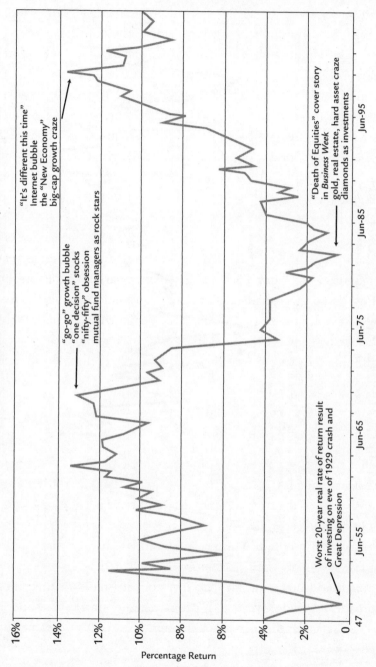

FOR STANDARD AND POOR'S 500, 1947–2004

Percentage Return

"It's different this time"
Internet bubble
the "New Economy"
big-cap growth craze

"go-go" growth bubble
"one decision" stocks
"nifty-fifty" obsession
mutual fund managers as rock stars

"Death of Equities" cover story
in *Business Week*
gold, real estate, hard asset craze
diamonds as investments

Worst 20-year real rate of return result
of investing on eve of 1929 crash and
Great Depression

16%

14%

12%

10%

8%

8%

4%

2%

0

47   Jun-55   Jun-65   Jun-75   Jun-85   Jun-95

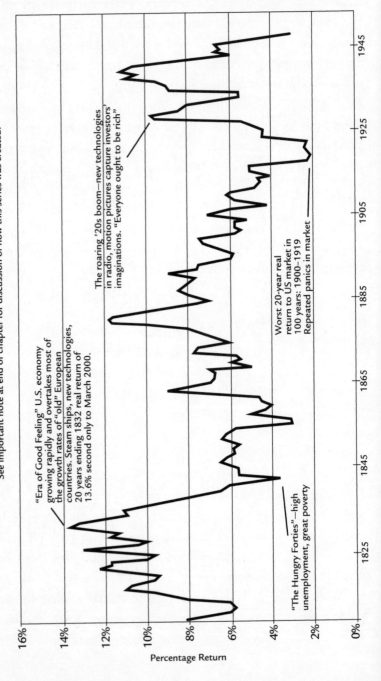

FIGURE 2-4 REAL ROLLING 20-YEAR COMPOUND AVERAGE ANNUAL RATES OF RETURN, 1809–1947

See important note at end of chapter for discussion of how this series was created.

most typical holding period is twenty years. Interestingly, this is
the same holding period that pension plans governed by ERISA
regulations use to make forecasts for the plan's anticipated returns.
Therefore, when reviewing historical returns a twenty-year holding period serves as an ideal starting point.

Figure 2–3 shows the S&P 500's real rolling rate of return
from June 30, 1927, through December 31, 2004. It's *exactly* the
same data that was used to generate figure 2–2, but broken down
into overlapping twenty-year holding periods. Thus, each dot represents the real rate of return for the S&P 500 for the prior twenty
years, with all periods overlapping. The average real twenty-year
rate of return to the S&P 500 over the 691 periods between June
1947 and December 2004 is 7.3 percent, very close to the real 7
percent rate of return seen between 1927 and 2004.

The 7 Percent Magnet

Seven percent emerges as an almost ironclad average for all longer
market return sequences. In Jeremy Siegel's *Stocks for the Long Run*,
for example, he looks at long subperiods of time and finds return
patterns that stray only a few basis points from that 7 percent average. Between 1802 and 1870, the real rate of return was 7.0 percent. Between 1871 and 1925, the return is 6.6 percent. Between
1926 and 2004, the return is 6.9 percent. And as we see in figure
2–4, when we extend the real twenty-year rates of return back to
1809, the figure remains 7.2 percent. This shows us that regardless
of what long period of time you analyze, the longer-term real return of 7 percent exerts a near gravitational pull on all long-term
stock market performance.

What figure 2–3 also shows quite clearly is that investors
swing from irrational exuberance to despondency and back again
with a fairly predictable degree of regularity. These empirical data,

as well as those featured in figure 2–4, show strong mean reversion and are consistent with financial models that posit inefficient stock prices, where investors irrationally reward popular stocks with unsustainable valuations, driving market prices to levels that have little relation to fundamental values. In chapter 6 we'll see that much of this can be explained through the lens of behavioral finance, which finds investors to be decidedly less rational than classical economic models assume.

The data are unequivocal—whenever real long-term returns get considerably higher than 7 percent, they spend the next twenty years trending back toward it, often overshooting the mark and falling a good bit below it. On the other hand, whenever they fall significantly below 7 percent they spend the next twenty years rising back toward it. The historical data also clearly show that the range of returns around that 7 percent mean can be quite extreme: The S&P 500's lowest twenty-year real compound average annual rate of return was 0.29 percent for the twenty years ending August 31, 1949, the result of investing right before the stock market crash in 1929 and suffering through the ensuing Great Depression. The S&P 500's highest real rate of return was 13.85 percent for the twenty years ending March 31, 2000.

Figure 2–3 tells a much different story from the one most investors are familiar with. While the S&P 500's average twenty-year real return might be 7 percent, the market routinely offers investors returns both well above and below that figure and does so in a very cyclic manner.

Lest you think that this is only a twentieth-century phenomenon, look at figure 2–4. Using annual data from Roger G. Ibbotson and Gary P. Brinson's book *Investment Markets: Gaining the Performance Advantage,* I created a hypothetical index of real rates of U.S. stock returns for all rolling twenty-year periods from 1809 through 1947, when the newer Ibbotson data takes over (see the note at the end of this chapter for how this index was generated). The chart is virtually identical to the twentieth-century chart, showing us that the market has vacillated between being overvalued and undervalued for nearly two hundred years, and has done so with a remarkable degree of consistency.

A Closer Look at the Last Seventy-eight Years

When we look closely at figure 2–3, we see investors' moods alternating between despair and elation; in every era investors let the previous twenty years dictate their outlook for the next twenty years. Let's start by looking at the late 1940s, when the market was emerging from the worst twenty-year period for real rates of return in the twentieth century, the result of investing on the eve of the stock market crash and depression of the 1930s.

According to John Dennis Brown's *101 Years on Wall Street,* "the nation's investors had become so traumatized by a Depression mindset by 1949 that even *Life* magazine, in an unlikely feature published in March, pointed out the pathetic level of stock prices as measured against fundamentals like earnings, dividends, and cash in the till." At the time, equities were seen as such speculative investments that many pension plans were barred from buying them. The entire generation was horribly scarred by the experiences of the Depression and extremely pessimistic about the future of the stock market.

My father remembers a conversation he had with my grandfather—a successful entrepreneur—in the late 1940s about the dangers that lurked on Wall Street. At the time, my father and his brothers were trying to talk my grandfather into investing in the stock market, citing the dirt cheap prices, low PE ratios, and high dividend yields that even the bluest of blue-chip stocks offered to investors. My grandfather's response was a vehement and thunderous No! The previous twenty years had taught him that only a fool would invest money in stocks, and he carried this attitude with him to his grave. He viewed Wall Street with deep suspicion, seeing unsuspecting new investors being suckered into rigged stock pools and fools who bought stocks on 10 percent margin. His was a common view for men his age who had made it through the Depression. The stock market crash so scarred their psyches that it would go on to define the way they would invest for the rest of their lives. Indeed, in 1940 the NYSE's trading volume was less than it had been in 1905, and fear of another depression that many believed would follow World War II kept a lid on any price improvement for many years.

For people my father's age, however, the stock market was looking better and better. In their thirties, he and his brothers saw the world much differently—for a number of reasons. Stock valuations were lower than they had been in decades, the creation of the SEC and other regulatory bodies gave them confidence in the market's integrity, the United States had won World War II, and speculation about a postwar depression proved unfounded. My father's generation saw a new world order emerging, with the United States at its center. And so the reversion to the long-term 7 percent mean began.

In the 1950s, stock market returns were higher than they had been in more than a generation. As a result, the public's attitude about the market began to improve. As older investors who remembered the speculative mania of the 1920s and the ensuing depression began to die off, new investors with shorter memories replaced them. Buying manias appeared once again, the likes of which had not been seen since the bull market of the 1920s. Between 1957 and 1959, investors drove the prices of the era's technology darlings—like Haloid-Xerox, Texas Instruments, Fairchild Camera, Polaroid, and IBM—sky high. In just two years, Texas Instruments' stock soared from $16 to $194 per share. (Sound familiar?) Yet all of this was just a prelude of things to come. Market speculation would push real twenty-year rates of return higher than 13 percent and usher in a new attitude—an outlook eerily similar to that in 1929.

The Soaring Sixties

By the late 1960s, the depression mindset had been swept aside. All the talk was of the new economy, a new world order, and a new era for permanently high stock market valuations. (Again, sound familiar?) Investors believed Keynesian economic models would make the economic cycle obsolete and that the government, in its infinite wisdom, would be able to fine-tune the economy, thereby leaving the stock market at permanently high plateaus. The years 1967 and 1968 were the most speculative in the market since 1929, with the American Stock Exchange—the NASDAQ of its era—experiencing the greatest speculation.

Dubbed the "go-go growth" era, the late 1960s were remarkably similar to the late 1990s. Back then, portfolio managers were treated like rock stars and investors believed that a handful of stocks known as the "nifty-fifty" were all you needed to get rich. They were called "one-decision stocks" because the only decision you had to make was to buy them—and watch the profits roll in. Comprising companies like Xerox, IBM, Coca-Cola, Polaroid, and ITT, they were the premier large-cap growth stocks of their era. All of them had remarkable growth records and huge market capitalizations. They made up the core holdings of institutional portfolios and were the darlings of the big money managers.

But the "nifty-fifty" were not the only objects of investors' desires. Computer and technology stocks soared—in 1967 alone, Memorex jumped from $62 to $226 per share and Control Data quintupled from $34 to $166. And those were the blue chips of the technology sector—smaller, more speculative stocks increased ten- to twenty-fold in a few short years.

According to the book *101 Years on Wall Street,* "the year 1967 was a vintage year for speculators. About 45 percent of all issues listed at the New York Stock Exchange would gain 50 percent or more." Despite the great political upheaval of the time—civil rights riots, anti-Vietnam protests, and flower children flocking to San Francisco to tune in and drop out—the market soared ever higher toward its apex in 1968. Between 1966 and 1968, the American Stock Exchange's return was six times that of the Dow, and investors believed they were living in a golden era in which markets would never decline.

The Morning After

Alas, it was not to be. After one more valiant attempt at the old highs, the market went into a freefall in 1973, ushering in the biggest bear market since the 1930s. To make matters worse, inflation rose unabated, silently robbing investors of even the meager returns they were earning. The grand plans of Keynesian economics came unglued in the 1970s, with unemployment *and* inflation soaring, the government recklessly printing money, and the entire economic underpinnings of the new era coming apart at the seams.

The "nifty-fifty" collapsed—as one *Forbes* columnist noted, "they were taken out and shot one by one." From their highs in the early 1970s to their lows near the market's bottom in 1974, Xerox fell 71 percent, Avon 86 percent, and Polaroid 91 percent. An entire generation of investors was reminded that valuations *did* matter and that you could be crushed if you believed that large-cap stocks could consistently be valued at one hundred times earnings. And it wasn't just the hot stocks of the day that were decimated—between 1968 and 1982, the S&P 500 lost a total of 10 percent, with every dollar invested on December 31, 1968, worth just 90 cents fifteen years later.

As they had in the late 1940s, investors came to hate the prospects for the stock market. Hard assets such as gold and silver, real estate, commodities, and oil and gas tax shelters became the rage. On August 13, 1979, *BusinessWeek* ran a cover story called "The Death of Equities," in which they said:

> The masses long ago switched from stocks to investments having higher yields and more protection from inflation. Now the pension funds—the market's last hope—have won permission to quit stocks and bonds for real estate, futures, gold, and even diamonds. The death of equities looks like an almost permanent condition—reversible, someday, but not soon. . . . At least 7 million shareholders have defected from the stock market since 1970, leaving equities more than ever the province of giant institutional investors. And now the institutions have been given the go-ahead to shift more of their money from stocks—and bonds—into other investments. If the institutions, who control the bulk of the nation's wealth, now withdraw billions from both the stock and bond markets, the implications for the US economy could not be worse . . . the problem is not merely that there are 7 million fewer shareholders than there were in 1970. Younger investors, in particular, are avoiding stocks. Between 1970 and 1975, the number of investors declined in every age group, but one: individuals 65 and older. While the number of investors under 65 dropped by about 25 percent, the number of investors over 65 jumped by more than 30 percent. Only the elderly who have not understood the changes in the nation's financial markets, or who are unable to adjust to them, are sticking with stocks.

The magazine goes on to say that "Wall Street has learned that there are more profitable things besides stocks to sell, among them options, futures, and real estate that it did not have in the 1950s. For better or for worse, then, the U.S. economy probably has to regard the death of equities as a near permanent condition." The article finishes with a quote from Alan B. Coleman, dean of Southern Methodist University's business school, who says: "we have entered a new financial age. The old rules no longer apply."

The Internet Bubble

All of which brings us to the era we are most familiar with—the Internet and technology bubble of the late 1990s. Here too, investors passionately believed that the old rules no longer applied. It featured the same mantras, the same hopes, the same dreams, and the same outlandish valuations as the bubble of the 1960s. The only investment you needed to make was in anything.com or businesses even vaguely associated with Silicon Valley. The new economy would displace the old; page views and user eyeballs would replace earnings and dividends as valuation metrics; B2B, B2C, and the "killer app" would permanently replace the old economy. The refrain "it's different this time" was on everyone's lips and in everyone's hearts. Investors of the 1990s made the speculative 1960s look positively quaint. In the earlier mania, investors had priced earnings at merely one hundred times the stock price: investors of the late 1990s pushed PE ratios into the stratosphere, awarding favorite companies like America Online a PE ratio of 635!

Countless articles about the stock market's ascent claimed that we had never seen such a mighty bull market, and that our own era was truly unique and electrifying. In 1998 and 1999 in particular, a frenzy infected investors, clouding their judgment and paralyzing their ability to reason. As we know now, it ended with a bang, not a whimper. The ensuing bear market was more fero-cious than any seen since the 1970s. Thus began the reversion—again—back to that 7 percent mean.

The Importance of the Starting Line

As Mark Twain once said, "The art of prophecy is very difficult, es-pecially with respect to the future." When using historical data to project future market returns, the first thing to consider is where the market currently stands in relation to the 7 percent mean. Nearly two hundred years of data show that equity markets al-ways revert to this long-term mean. Therefore, where you *start* in the process is very important when trying to determine where you will *end up*.

If you start in a market characterized by low valuations, rela-tively high dividend yields, and unspectacular previous twenty-year returns, your chance of doing very well over the next twenty years is quite high. Conversely, if you start in a market character-ized by high valuations, low dividend yields, and spectacular pre-vious twenty-year returns, you had best brace for a challenging twenty-year period ahead.

Table 2–2 summarizes the results achieved twenty years after the market has reached an extreme, and figures 2–5 and 2–6 show the frequency of returns at various levels. (I define "extreme" as be-ing one standard deviation above or below the average return of 7.3 percent; 68 percent of all returns fall within one standard de-viation, so we'll only look at the 32 percent of the time that re-turns exceed one standard deviation. This is a simple way of identifying returns that have strayed fairly far from the mean.)

For example, between June of 1947 and December of 2004 the average twenty-year real average annual return is 7.3 percent. The standard deviation of return for the entire period is 3.76 percent.

TABLE 2-2 RETURNS AFTER EXTREME
20-YEAR REAL RETURNS

	S&P 500 Real 20-Year CAGR	
	3.54% or Lower	11.06% or Higher
Number of Occurrences	130	95
Minimum Return, 20 years later	8.36%	0.55%
Maximum Return, 20 years later	13.85%	9.42%
Average Return, 20 years later	11.19%	2.63%
Median Return, 20 years later	11.53%	2.27%
All Time High	13.85%	Mar-00
Current	9.93%	Dec-04
Implied Real Return, 2022–2025	**3% to 5%**	

Thus, we'll examine times when market returns were *below* 3.54 percent (7.3 percent minus one standard deviation of 3.76 percent equals 3.54 percent) or *above* 11.06 percent (7.3 percent plus one standard deviation of 3.76 percent equals 11.06 percent) over the previous twenty years.

Investors hoping for strong returns from the S&P 500 over the next twenty years will find little comfort in this data. Since 1947, the S&P 500's rolling twenty-year real rate of return was one standard deviation above the mean ninety-five times. As you can see in table 2–2, when returns over the past twenty years were significantly higher than the long-term average, the average return twenty years later was a meager 2.63 percent, and 98 percent of all returns fall between zero and 4 percent!

On the other hand, when the previous twenty years served up disappointing returns the opposite occurs: for the 130 periods

FIGURE 2–5 HISTOGRAM OF FREQUENCY OF 20-YEAR REAL RETURNS AFTER LOW 20-YEAR RETURNS

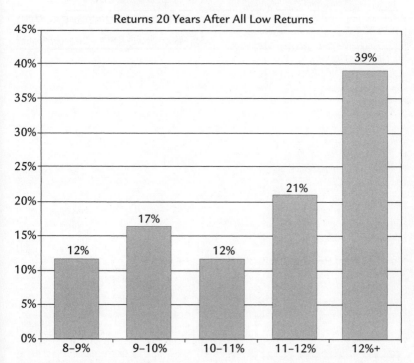

Returns 20 Years After All Low Returns

when the rolling twenty-year real rate of return was less than 3.53 percent, the *minimum* return twenty years later was 8.36 percent, the maximum was 13.85 percent, and the average was 11.19 percent. For investors lucky enough to start investing when the market was coming off a twenty-year dry spell, the returns twenty years later were *always* better than average.

The Importance of Valuation

When you look at tables 2–3 through 2–6, graciously supplied to me by the Leuthold Group, a Minneapolis-based quantitative

TABLE 2–3 NORMALIZED P/E RATIO FOR STANDARD AND POOR'S 500, 1926–2004

S&P 500
QUARTERLY AVERAGE
NORMALIZED P/E RATIOS
1926 TO DATE
316 QUARTERS
(304 excluding outliers)

S&P 500: P/E Ratios...Normalized
(5 Year Average Earnings)

1926 to Date
(Shaded Numbers Indicate Outliers)

Median
16.2x
↓

P/E Ratio	Quarters (shaded = outliers)
5.0	32-2
6.0	
7.0	32-1, 32-3, 32-4, 33-1
8.0	31-4, 82-1, 82-2, 82-3
8.5	42-2
9.0	42-1, 78-1, 78-4, 79-1, 79-2, 79-4, 80-1, 81-3
9.5	48-2, 48-3, 52-3, 53-3, 49-4, 54-1, 50-1, 50-2, 50-4, 51-1, 51-2, 51-3, 51-4, 52-1, 52-2, 52-4, 53-4, 74-4, 78-2, 79-3, 80-3, 81-2, 82-4
10.0	33-2, 41-4, 53-1, 54-2, 77-4, 78-3, 80-4, 81-1, 83-1, 84-2
10.5	41-2, 48-1, 41-3, 43-1, 54-2, 74-3, 77-3, 84-1, 84-3, 84-4
11.0	31-3, 48-3, 44-1, 75-1, 77-2, 83-2, 83-3, 83-4
11.5	43-4, 44-1, 48-4, 54-3
12.0	31-2, 38-2, 40-2, 40-4, 44-2, 85-3
12.5	44-3, 44-4, 48-1, 48-3, 75-2, 76-2, 85-2, 86-1
13.0	30-4, 39-2, 48-2, 54-4, 76-1, 76-3, 76-4
13.5	31-1, 33-3, 33-4, 39-3, 45-1, 48-2, 58-1, 85-4
14.0	26-2, 26-4, 27-1, 40-1, 47-4, 55-1, 58-2, 70-3, 74-4
14.5	26-3, 27-2, 37-4, 39-1, 45-2, 47-2, 47-3, 55-2, 57-1, 70-2
15.0	25-1, 45-3, 46-4, 47-1, 57-2, 57-3, 58-3, 74-4, 88-1
15.5	27-3, 58-4, 88-3
16.0	27-4, 28-1, 30-3, 55-3, 55-4, 58-1, 70-1, 70-4, 88-1, 88-2, 88-4, 90-4, 86-4, 89-2, 90-3
16.5	34-1, 56-2, 56-3, 58-4, 73-4, 86-2, 86-3, 87-4, 88-1
17.0	34-2, 34-4, 45-4, 59-1, 60-1, 60-2, 60-3, 60-4, 64-4, 69-4, 73-3

CURRENT STATUS
• January 14, 2005: 21.2x (83rd Percentile)
  —76th Percentile 1957 To Date
• 4th Quarter Average (Labeled 04-4): 21.5x
• Conclusion: Stocks Moderately Overvalued

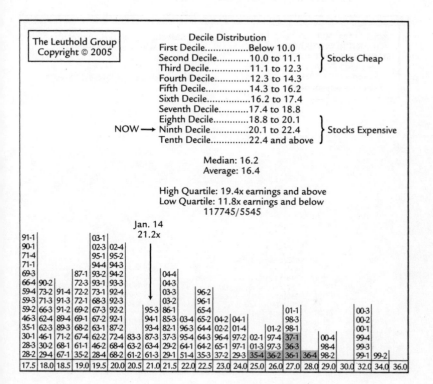

METHODOLOGY

• Normalizing: Earnings are far more cyclical than book value or dividends, so we think the use of a smoothing technique is essential for making comparisons. The normalizing technique employed for the S&P 500 takes a four and one-half year average of historical earnings along with two quarters of estimated future earnings.

• Adjusted Earnings: S&P 500 earnings have been adjusted in recent years to account for the big write-offs that companies have taken. Basically, adjusted earnings are the average of reported earnings and operating earnings. Adjustments go back to 1988.

• Outliers: In the early 1930s (P/E ratios less than eight) and in 1935—1937 (P/E ratios over 24), normalized earnings were warped by the Depression's virtual earnings wipe out. These twelve quarterly outliers (noted above by shading) are excluded from decile distribution and median and average calculations.

TABLE 2–4 DIVIDEND YIELD FOR
STANDARD AND POOR'S 500, 1926–2004

S&P 500: YIELDS QUARTERLY AVERAGE YIELDS 1926 TO DATE 316 QUARTERS (312 excluding outliers)	S&P 500: Yields 1926 to Date (Shaded Numbers Indicate Outliers)

Jan. 14
1.76%
↓

Histogram of quarterly average dividend yields, plotted by yield value (bottom axis). Each bucket lists the quarters (shown top → bottom in the stack):

Yield	Quarters (top → bottom of stack)
1.1	00-3
1.2	01-1, 00-4, 00-2, 00-1, 99-4, 99-3, 99-2
1.3	01-2, 99-1
1.4	02-1, 01-4, 98-4, 98-3, 98-2, 98-1
1.6	04-4, 04-3, 04-2, 04-1, 03-4, 03-3, 03-2, 02-3, 02-2, 97-4, 97-3
1.7	01-3, 03-1, 97-2, 97-1
1.9	96-4
2.0	
2.1	
2.2	96-3, 96-2
2.3	96-1
2.4	95-4
2.5	95-3
2.6	95-2
2.7	94-1, 93-4
2.8	95-1, 94-4, 94-3, 93-3, 93-2, 93-1, 87-3, 73-1, 72-4, 72-3, 72-2
2.9	94-2, 87-2, 72-1, 68-4, 64-3, 62-1, 61-4, 61-3, 61-2
3.0	92-4, 92-3, 92-2, 92-1, 87-1, 73-2, 66-3, 66-1, 65-4, 65-2, 65-1, 64-4, 64-2, 64-1
3.1	73-3, 71-3, 71-2, 69-2, 69-1, 68-2, 67-4, 67-3, 65-3, 63-4, 63-3, 61-1, 59-4, 59-3, 29-3
3.2	91-4, 91-3, 91-2, 71-4, 71-1, 68-1, 66-2, 59-2, 59-1
3.3	89-3, 73-4, 69-3, 67-1, 63-2, 62-2
3.4	90-2, 89-4, 86-4, 86-3, 86-2, 63-1, 58-4
3.5	91-1, 90-1, 89-2, 60-4, 60-3, 60-2, 60-1, 29-2, 29-1
3.6	89-1, 87-4, 74-1, 70-4, 70-1, 66-4, 66-3, 62-4, 62-3, 58-3
3.7	90-3, 88-4, 88-3, 88-2, 88-1, 86-1, 75-3, 75-2, 75-1, 67-2, 55-4, 46-2, 36-1, 35-4

CURRENT STATUS
- July 1, 2005: 1.86x (89th Percentile)
  —84th Percentile 1957 To Date
- 2nd Quarter Average (Labeled 05-2): 1.85%
- Conclusion: Stocks Overvalued
- T-bonds yield 2.4x stocks, quality corporates yield 2.8x.

The Leuthold Group
Copyright © 2005

Decile Distribution (excludes outliers)

First Decile................6.02% and above	⎫ Stocks
Second Decile............5.23% to 6.02%	⎬ Cheap
Third Decile................4.27% to 5.23%	⎭
Fourth Decile.............4.24% to 4.27%	
Fifth Decile................3.89% to 4.24%	
Sixth Decile...............3.60% to 3.89%	
Seventh Decile...........3.19% to 3.60%	
Eighth Decile.............2.96% to 3.19%	
Ninth Decile..............2.21% to 2.96%	⎫ Stocks
NOW → Tenth Decile..............Below 2.21%	⎬ Expensive

Median: 3.89%
Average: 4.08%

High Quartile: 5.02% and above
Low Quartile: 3.08% and below
117745/2085

Median 3.89% →

3.8	3.9	4.0	4.2	4.4	4.6	4.8	5.0	5.2	5.4	5.6	5.8	6.0	6.2	6.4	6.6	6.8	7.0	7.25	7.5	7.75	8.0	8.25	8.5	9.0
			85-3					91-3																
			85-2					80-1																
			83-4					79-3																
			83-3					79-2																
			83-2					79-1																
			77-1					78-4																
			76-4																					
			76-3	84-4				78-2																
			76-2	84-3				74-4																
			58-1	84-2			82-4	54-2																
			39-1	83-1			80-3	48-2																
			37-1	80-4	81-2		78-3	47-3																
	86-4	36-4		85-1	77-3	81-1	77-4	47-2	81-4			82-3												
	76-4	36-3		84-1	75-1	74-3	44-4	44-2	80-2			53-4												
	70-3	35-3		77-2	54-4	54-3	44-3	44-1	79-4			53-3												
	70-2	33-3		57-4	47-1	46-4	43-3	43-4	78-1			52-2				51-2								
56-2	90-4	68-2		55-1	39-3	45-1	43-2	40-1	63-1	54-1	82-1	52-1					50-3							
56-1	74-2	55-2	30-1	46-3	33-4	39-2	39-4	35-1	48-3	52-4	53-2	51-4				51-3	50-1	51-1	42-3	50-4				
55-3	57-1	46-3	29-4	46-2	30-3	37-2	37-3	27-1	38-3	47-4	52-3	48-4	42-4			50-2	49-3	49-4	41-2	41-4				
46-1	46-4	36-2	28-3	34-2	27-4	35-2	34-4	26-4	33-2	43-1	30-4	48-1	40-4			49-1	41-3	49-2	38-1	38-2	42-2			32-2
28-4	38-4	34-1	28-2	28-1	27-3	34-3	27-2	26-3	26-1	31-1	26-2	40-2	31-2	31-3	40-3	41-1	37-4	32-4	33-1		42-1	32-3	31-4	32-1

METHODOLOGY

• Dividends: Based on trailing 12 month dividend rate for the S&P 500 as reported in *Barron's*.

• Payout ratio for S&P 500 is currently at about 36.8%. This decreased slightly from last quarter's 37.1%, as dividends have grown at a slightly lower rate than earnings.

• Outliers: High yields in early 1930s are misleading and prevailed only momentarily, as dividends were cut sharply during the Depression. Those four outliers have been excluded from the decile distribution and calculation of the median and average on the 1926 to date histogram.

• Overvalued Range: Note that on the decile distributions, stocks are considered to be overvalued only in the ninth and tenth deciles. Stocks are viewed as cheap in the first three deciles.

FIGURE 2–6 HISTOGRAM OF FREQUENCY OF RETURNS AFTER HIGH 20-YEAR RETURNS

Returns 20 Years After All High Returns

consulting and asset management company, you see that it is not reversion to the mean alone that drives the process. Low PE ratios and high dividend yields are also important precursors to rising markets. Over all twenty-year periods analyzed, bull markets started when PE ratios fell into the bottom two deciles (the 20 percent of the time when the market was the cheapest) and when the S&P 500's dividend yield was much higher than average.

The year 1982 is a great example. Because of its anemic performance over the previous twenty years, people were uniformly negative on the stock market, fearing the bad news would never end. At the time, the S&P 500 had a very low PE ratio of 8 and a very healthy dividend yield of 6 percent. The market was only cheaper in the 1930s, right before it went romping to double-digit returns.

Conversely, when you look at periods when the market was

posting huge twenty-year performance numbers, you see that valuations were indicating it was vastly overpriced. During the soaring sixties, for example, PE ratios consistently landed in the tenth decile (the most expensive) and dividend yields fell in the ninth and tenth deciles (the lowest yields).

TABLE 2–5 RETURNS FOR STANDARD AND POOR'S 500 10 YEARS AFTER HIGH AND LOW P/E RATIOS, 1926–2005 (RETURNS ARE NOMINAL)

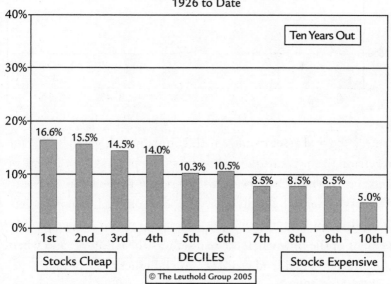

Median Ten-Year Annual Compound Total Returns
from Historical P/E Deciles
1926 to Date

© The Leuthold Group 2005

Over a 10-year time horizon, the message is that buying the stock market at historically high P/E levels (9th and 10th deciles) produces significantly lower long-term performance. Even after 10 years, time won't bail you out of the performance hole.

• Today's market level (9th decile of this distribution) has typically produced 10-year total return performance of 8.5% per year (including dividends). This is well below the 12%–13% average annual stock market total return over this 1926 to date time frame.

TABLE 2-6 RETURNS FOR STANDARD AND POOR'S 500 10 YEARS AFTER HIGH AND LOW DIVIDEND YIELD, 1926–2005 (RETURNS ARE NOMINAL)

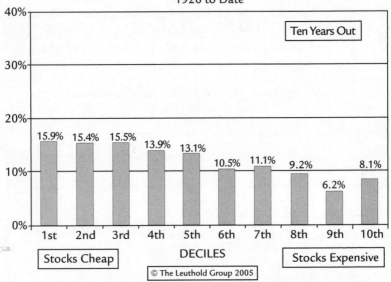

Median Ten-Year Annual Compound Total Returns
from Historic Yield Deciles
1926 to Date

© The Leuthold Group 2005

Over a 10-year time horizon, it is obvious that future returns typically decline relative to the prevailing yield level. It is best to buy stocks when yields are high (decile 1, 2, and 3).

• Today's market level (10th decile of this distribution) has typically produced 10-year performance of 8.1% per year. Not too bad, but about 3% of the annual gain came from dividends.

The Leuthold Group maintains similar studies ranking the market's valuations against historical averages. Each study finds that when the market starts from high price-to-book, price-to-cash flow, and price-to-sales ratios or high percentage of gross domestic product, returns over the long term are *low*. Conversely, when these same ratios are low, subsequent long-term returns are *high*.

In my book *What Works on Wall Street*, I found the same applied to individual stocks. Over time, investors who buy stocks and indexes with very high valuations wind up performing horribly, while investors who buy low are richly rewarded.

So what does the market look like right now? In the first quarter of 2005—even *after* the bear market of 2000–2002—the S&P 500's PE ratio was a high 21.3 and its dividend yield a low 1.84 percent, both falling in the ninth deciles. Despite the bear market, the stocks in the S&P 500 are still very expensive by historical standards.

S&P 500 Forecasting Models

To fully test the theory that reversion to the mean and valuation models can accurately forecast the S&P 500's returns over the next twenty years, I looked at three traditional models analysts use to forecast the market's long-term expected rate of return. The results are featured in table 2–7.

The first model is the widely used market implied expected rate of return for equities. This is derived by adding the earnings yield of the market (earnings divided by price, or the inverse of the PE ratio) to the market's dividend yield. This model tells you what investors expect to earn from the market over time, subtracting anticipated inflation to arrive at the real expected rate of return. As I write this in the summer of 2005, this model predicts an expected real long-term rate of return of 4.78 percent.

The next model I reviewed is the well-known Capital Asset Pricing Model. This academic model adds the equity risk premium to the prevailing riskless rate of return (commonly the twenty-year Treasury bond yield, here the yield on the inflation-protected Treasury bond). This model predicts a fairly high real expected rate of return of 7.10 percent, very close to the long-term average.

TABLE 2-7 TRADITIONAL FORECASTING RESULTS FOR THE STANDARD AND POOR 500

Market Implied Real Expected Rate of Return for Equities

Earnings Yield		Dividend Yield		Expected Rate of Return		Inflation[1]	Real Expected Real Return
5.97%	+	1.81%	=	7.78%	−	3%	4.78%

Capital Asset Pricing Model

Inflation-Adjusted Treasury[2]		Beta		Equity Risk Premium[3]		Real Expected Rate of Return
1.70%	+	(1	x	5.4%)	=	7.10%

Equity Cost of Capital (Dividend Discount Model)

Current Dividend Yield		Expected Dividend Growth[4]		Expected Rate of Return		Inflation	Real-Expected Rate of Return
1.81%	+	7.00%	=	8.81%	−	3%	5.81%

Notes:
1. Long-term average for inflation.
2. Yield on 20-year inflation-protected U.S. Treasury bond.
3. Equity risk premium derived by Dimson, Marsh and Staunton of London Business School using 101 years of world market returns.
4. *Value Line* estimates for 500 stocks in S&P 500.

This is not too surprising, since this model assumes that the equity risk premium is static. The problem with this approach, however, is getting the expected equity risk premium right. In theory, *stocks* should provide greater returns than safe investments like *Treasury bonds*. This difference is called the *equity risk premium*—it's the excess return that you earn by taking more risk. The problem is that over time, the equity risk premium has varied considerably, and like the 7 percent real rate of return to the market, you can't assume that you will always be getting the historical average. Over all rolling twenty-year periods, we see that the equity risk premium averages 7.19 percent, but has been as high as 15.51 percent and as low as 0.23 percent.

In trying to determine which prospective risk premium was most accurate, I turned to the marvelous *Triumph of the Optimists: 101 Years of Global Investment Returns* by Elroy Dimson, Paul Marsh, and Mike Staunton. The authors analyze the returns in sixteen countries over the last 101 years. In chapter 13 of the book, they offer a very well thought out argument for using a prospective risk premium of 5.4 percent, a figure that I will use here. Keep in mind, however, that this number varies over time and requires the *very* large assumption that the risk premium will continue to be 5.4 percent over the next twenty years. Nevertheless, this becomes our high estimate from the traditional models.

The third and final forecasting model I use is the well-known Equity Cost of Capital, or dividend discount model. This model adds the market's current dividend yield to the expected dividend growth rate over the next five years. (I use the *Value Line Investment Survey*'s forecast for projected dividend growth.) Thus, when you add the current dividend yield of 1.81 percent to the forecasted dividend growth rate of 7 percent and then remove inflation, you arrive at a forecast for a real rate of return of 5.81 percent.

Finally, to arrive at a careful estimate for future returns, I take an average of the three models. The result? An expected rate of return of 5.90 percent, just one percentage point shy of mean reversion alone.

The S&P 500's Twenty-Year Outlook

Large stocks have recently achieved their highest real rate of return in history: 13.85 percent for the twenty years ending March 31, 2000. Using reversion to the mean statistics, valuation metrics, and the combination of the three traditional forecasting models discussed above, I expect that non-style-specific large stocks will be poor performers in the coming twenty years. If the market continues to behave as it has over the last two hundred years, exhibiting the same reversion to the mean as it has in the past, we can assume that the *best*-case scenario for the S&P 500 through 2020–2025 is a real average annual return between 3 and 5 percent. Keep in mind that this is a forecast for only broad cap-weighted indexes like the S&P 500. Luckily, we'll see in the next few chapters that the twenty-year outlook for *other* strategy-based indexes and style- and cap-tilted indexes is much more optimistic.

Chapter Two Highlights

◆ Investors mistakenly assume they can use the nominal, seventy-eight-year average return as a good proxy for what to expect over shorter periods of time. This has led many to assume they will continue to earn between 10 and 15 percent annually in their equity portfolios.

◆ Investors confuse nominal and real returns. Real returns are what matter, since they take inflation into account. You should always focus on the growth of your purchasing power rather than the nominal increase in your portfolio.

◆ Investors should review all rolling periods that match their anticipated holding period. Most investors saving and investing for their retirement should focus on the returns in all rolling twenty-year periods.

◆ When looking at the S&P 500, the disparity of real rates of return in all rolling twenty-year periods is very wide, ranging from a twenty-year real return of 0.29 percent to 13.85 percent. The average is 7.2 percent.

◆ Evidence for the past two hundred years is unequivocal—markets revert to their long-term mean. Periods when returns are substantially below average are typically followed by high rates of return and periods that are substantially above average are typically followed by low rates of return.

◆ Reversion to the mean, valuation, and traditional forecasting models converge on a forecasted expected real rate of return of 3 to 5 percent a year for the S&P 500 and other large-cap weighted broad indexes.

◆ Style-neutral indexing (like investing in the S&P 500) was a great way to invest over the last twenty years, but will be one of the worst over the next twenty years.

Note on the construction of the equity return series in figure 2–4 (page 28):

The rolling twenty-year real rate of return to U.S. equity markets featured in figure 2–4 was constructed using calendar year-end annual data from the book *Investment Markets: Gaining the Performance Advantage,* by Roger G. Ibbotson and Gary P. Brinson (McGraw-Hill, 1987). In chapter 5, pages 65 through 86, Ibbotson and Brinson supply the nominal stock market total returns for various portfolios. For the period 1790 through 1871, they use a composite portfolio derived from the Foundation for the Study of

Cycles, Pittsburgh. The foundation uses its internal index for 1789 to June 1831; the Cleveland Trust Co. railroad stock index for July 1831 to February 1854; the Clement-Burgess Index from March 1854 to July 1871; and the Cowles Index for August to December 1871. These indices, except for the Cowles Index, may suffer from survivorship bias, which means that firms that fail are not considered, biasing returns upward, and from other indeterminate biases. For the period 1926 through 2004, I use the returns for the S&P 500 and inflation as supplied by Ibbotson EnCorr Analyzer.

To transform the nominal series to real rates of return for the period 1790 through 1926, I subtracted from each year's return the decade's average for inflation for that time period. Thus, for the period 1790 through 1926, actual inflation on an annual basis is not available, but the average inflation for that decade is substituted. For the period 1926 through 2004, actual monthly inflation figures are used. The formula used to calculate real rates of return is: real rate of return = $((1+\text{Asset Return})/(1+\text{Inflation})) - 1$.

3

Salvation from Small Stocks

History is a better guide than good intentions.

—Jeane Kirkpatrick

Lucky for us—given the rather meager prospects for the S&P 500—the market is made up of more than large-cap stocks. Small-cap stocks are the little engines that could, and as we'll see in this chapter, hold much greater promise than large-cap stocks in the coming twenty years. Traditionally, small-cap stocks are those with market capitalizations between $200 million and $2 billion. Stocks with capitalizations below $200 million are micro-caps, which most institutional portfolio managers remove from consideration when buying small-cap stocks because of their large bid-ask spreads and resulting trading illiquidity. Typically, once a stock's market cap rises above $200 million, bid-ask prices decline and liquidity improves dramatically.

Table 3-1 breaks down the equity market by market capitalization and shows the number of issues available in each category.

The list includes only stocks with enough liquidity to be broadly purchased. Interestingly, while large-cap stocks make up nearly 75 percent of the market's capitalization there are only 368 stocks in the category, but there are thousands of stocks in the small- and mid-cap categories that make up the remaining 25 percent of the equity market.

TABLE 3–1 INVESTABLE U.S. STOCK UNIVERSE: ALL STOCKS IN COMPUSTAT DATABASE WITH AVERAGE LIQUIDITY OF $500,000 PER DAY, APRIL 2005

	Micro-Cap	Small-Cap	Mid-Cap	Large-Cap	Total
Capitalization in Millions	$0–$200	$200–$2000	$2000–$10000	$10000+	
Number of Companies	488	1988	741	368	3585
Percentage of Total Market Capitalization	0.30%	7.94%	16.97%	74.79%	100%

If you wanted your portfolio to simply mirror the market, you would invest 75 percent in large-cap stocks, and 25 percent in small- and mid-cap issues. Most investors' portfolios are even more heavily skewed to large-cap stocks, with just a tiny percentage invested in the more populous small- and mid-cap categories.

Small Stocks Generally Outperform Large Stocks

In the past, small-cap stocks have performed significantly better than their large-cap brethren. Happily, we also have historical data on small-cap stocks, enabling us to analyze their performance in the same way we analyzed the performance of large-cap stocks. To study the performance of smaller stocks, I use the Ibbotson U.S. inflation-adjusted Small Stocks Index. (Details on how this index is constructed and calculated can be found in the note at the end of this chapter.)

Figure 3–1 shows the terminal value of one dollar invested in both large- and small-cap stocks from June 30, 1927, through December 31, 2004. As in chapter 2, I am using real, not nominal returns, thereby taking the effects of inflation into account. Over those seventy-eight years, small-cap stocks did approximately four times better than large-cap stocks, turning one dollar into $1,058, a real average annual compound return of 9.4 percent. The higher returns, however, come at a price—small stocks are historically more volatile than large stocks, making investors suffer through a wilder ride as payback for the higher returns.

Why Small Stocks Have a Performance Advantage

Small-cap stocks have a performance advantage over large stocks for a variety of reasons. Primary among them is the *neglected firm effect*. Because there are thousands of stocks in this category, many are not widely followed by Wall Street's analysts. Smaller stocks are therefore less likely to be as efficiently priced as the more exhaustively researched large-cap stocks. When you have fewer analysts researching a company's or industry's prospects, it's much more likely for great earnings and growth potential to go unnoticed. This, in turn, creates buying opportunities for savvy investors.

Another reason small-cap stocks outperform larger stocks is simply *because* they are smaller. A company with $200 million in revenues is far more likely to be able to double those revenues than a company with $200 billion in revenues. With large companies, each increase in revenues becomes a smaller and smaller percentage of overall revenues. Small stocks, on the other hand, have

FIGURE 3–1

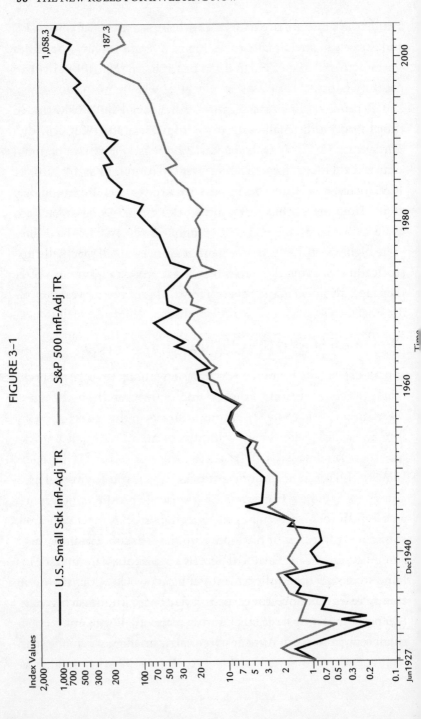

a much easier time delivering great percentage growth in revenues and earnings.

Figure 3–2 shows the real twenty-year average annual compound returns of large- and small-cap stocks between June 1947 and December 2004. As the graph shows, small-cap stocks traditionally outperform large-cap stocks in most twenty-year periods. The average small-cap real rate of return for all twenty-year periods analyzed is 10.42 percent. The *best* twenty-year real rate of return of 17.91 percent occurred during the twenty years ending June 30, 1952. The *worst* twenty-year real rate of return was 3.62 percent, which occurred during the twenty years ending November 30, 1948.

Note how much better the worst-case scenario is for small-cap stock returns. Large-cap stocks had two twenty-year periods where they did little better than break even, yet the *worst* twenty-year period for small-cap stocks still doubled an investor's money. Small stocks so consistently beat large stocks that researchers have come to believe that there should be a premium paid to people who invest in small-cap stocks. For example, over the 691 rolling twenty-year periods, small stocks outperformed the S&P 500 84 percent of the time.

The Small-Cap Premium

When you look at all rolling twenty-year periods between 1947 and 2004, you see that on average small-cap stocks compound at a premium of 3.12 percent over large-cap stocks. That may not sound like much, but it really adds up over time. For example, assume two investors have $10,000 IRA accounts; one invests in large stocks and the other invests in small stocks. Over the next twenty years each investor earns an average return for each group (7.3 percent for the large stock investor and 10.42 percent for the small stock investor). After twenty years, the large stock investor

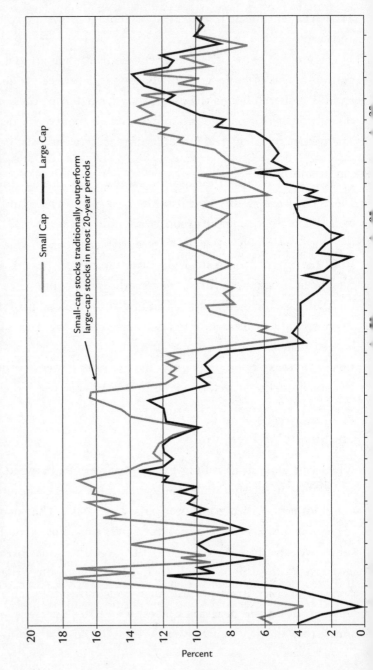

FIGURE 3–2 REAL ROLLING 20-YEAR AVERAGE ANNUAL COMPOND RETURNS, LARGE STOCKS AND SMALL STOCKS, JUNE 1947–DECEMBER 2004

would have a portfolio worth $40,926 but the small stock investor would have $72,603! See? That 3.12 percent adds up.

But as figure 3–3 also shows, the small-cap premium has historically been quite variable—while it averages 3.12 percent for all twenty-year periods, it has been as low as −3.09 percent and as high as 8.89 percent. Looking at figure 3–4, we see that the small-cap premium has an *inverse* relationship with large-cap stocks' total returns: when large stocks are doing particularly well, the small-cap premium is low or negative, and when large stocks are performing poorly, the small-cap premium is usually above its long-term average. For example, during the market bubble in the mid-1960s, the small-cap premium was nonexistent, with small stocks doing worse than large stocks over the previous twenty years. Conversely, if you look at the early 1980s when large stocks were struggling to offer *any* returns whatsoever, the small-cap premium was above 8 percent.

This point is extremely important to keep in mind when projecting where small stocks might go over the next twenty years. When you look at figure 3–4, you see that, on a relative basis, the twenty years ending March 31, 1999, was the worst period for small-cap stocks in history, with the largest gap between large stocks' returns and the small-cap premium *ever*. Reversion to the mean suggests that these two paths will cross again, as large stocks' performance heads down toward its historical mean and small-cap stocks' performance heads back up toward its historical premium. This has already begun—as of December 2004, the small-cap stock premium is once again in positive territory.

Further proof can be found during the period between 1968 and 1982, the last time large-cap stocks did poorly for an extended period of time. Over that same time period, small-cap stocks held their own. Between December 31, 1968, and December 31, 1982, an investment in the S&P 500 had a real rate of return of −1.06 percent

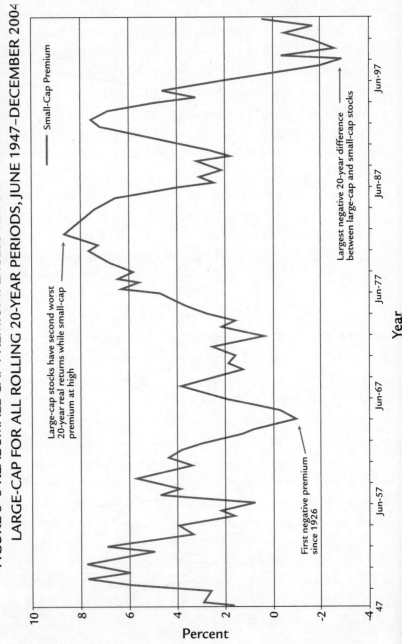

FIGURE 3-3 REAL SMALL-CAP PREMIUM: EXCESS RETURN OF SMALL-CAP STOCKS LARGE-CAP FOR ALL ROLLING 20-YEAR PERIODS, JUNE 1947–DECEMBER 2004

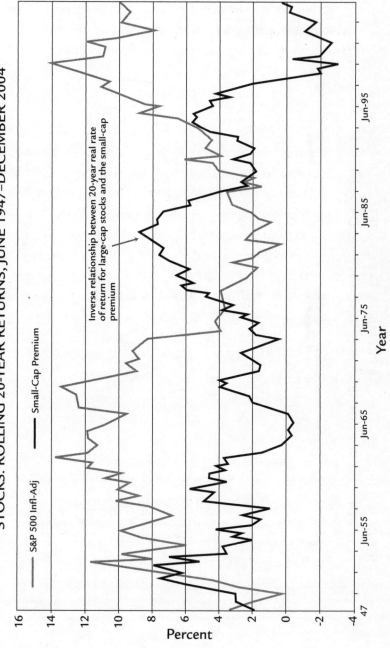

FIGURE 3-4 REAL SMALL-CAP PREMIUM VERSUS REAL TOTAL RETURNS FOR LARGE-CAP STOCKS. ROLLING 20-YEAR RETURNS, JUNE 1947–DECEMBER 2004

S&P 500 Infl-Adj — Small-Cap Premium

Inverse relationship between 20-year real rate of return for large-cap stocks and the small-cap premium per year, turning a one dollar investment made at the end of 1968 into just 86 cents fourteen years later. An investment in small stocks, however, compounded at a real rate of 3.65 percent over the same period, turning one dollar into $1.66 by the end of 1982.

The Pitfalls of Real Time

It's much easier singing the praises of small-cap stocks in 2005 than it was in 1999, however. I issued my first call for the excellent long-term prospects of small-cap stocks on January 1, 1999, in an article published on my company's Web site called "Looking Back to the Future: History Says Buy Small Stocks Now." Back then, small stocks had performed abysmally compared to the sizzling performance of large-cap growth and technology stocks. They were truly the ugly ducklings of most investors' portfolios. Many respected advisors thought that investors would be better off *totally excluding* small-cap stocks from their portfolios! Here's what I wrote then:

> Since 1994, the stock market has been extraordinarily bi-
> ased toward big-cap growth stocks. Virtually all of the returns
> generated by the S&P 500 this year are due to the stunning per-
> formance of just a handful of big growth stocks—the top 10 per-
> formers in the index accounted for 56% of the S&P 500's
> returns through the end of November. If your large-cap stock
> wasn't a Microsoft, Pfizer or Lucent, chances are it was flat for
> the year. As for stocks outside the big-cap growth arena, this
> year's market has been a virtual wasteland. Value and small-
> cap stocks have suffered terribly. . . . And if you want to see
> really bad, all you have to do is take a look at small-cap stocks.
> Those laggard big-cap value strategies look positively wonderful
> when compared to the plight of small-cap stocks. The small-cap

Russell is down more than 7% as of December 24, 1998. And even that figure masks the true shellacking the average small stock has endured—25% of the stocks in the Russell are down more than 50% from their highs this year! And if you look at our O'Shaughnessy Small-Cap Universe (7,964 stocks with market-caps below $1 billion), you'll see a median loss of 15.07% between January 1, 1998 and November 30, 1998.

With this sad state of affairs in the value and small cap categories, some wonderful opportunities have been created. The PE differential between the Russell and the S&P 500 is at an historic low of .78 (it usually trades at a much higher premium of 1.1 or more). This means small-cap stocks are extremely cheap compared to large-cap growth stocks. Unfortunately, most investors focus on the trees rather than the forest. They look at what has performed best recently—and expect the trend to continue. Rarely do they study the past—and look what happened after big stocks have had their run. And that is the strategic investor's crucial advantage. *By looking at history, we know that the last time large stocks outperformed small stocks for a -20-year period, the small fry went on to dominate for years. Since 1928, there were only four 20-year periods (out of a possible 51) when small stocks lagged large stocks. Someone understanding this important historic relationship between small and large stocks would see that small stocks are a great opportunity right now.*

Let's say you know that, over 20-year periods, small stocks almost never do worse than large stocks. And let's say you use such an occurrence as a signal to buy small stocks aggressively. The first time small stocks lagged large stocks for 20 years was in 1964. Over the ensuing 4 years, small stocks' performance exploded. Look at these returns:

Year	S&P 500	Ibbotson Small Stock Index	Difference
1965	12.45%	41.75%	+29.30%
1966	−10.06%	−7.01%	+3.05%
1967	23.98%	83.57%	+59.95%
1968	11.06%	35.97%	+25%

Someone investing $10,000 in small stocks at the start of 1965 would have $32,901 at the end of 1968, a gain of 229% in just four years! The same $10,000 invested in the S&P 500 returned a comparatively modest 39%, with $10,000 growing to just $13,926.

I find the current valuations of small stocks extremely compelling. But no one rings a bell and announces it's time for us to move from big-cap growth stocks to small-cap stocks. It takes foresight and courage to buck the big-cap growth trend, yet that is what history is telling us to do. So, as if on cue for our investment philosophy, Winston Churchill said: "The further backward you can look, the farther forward you are likely to see."

While I will address the psychological ramifications of this article in chapter 6, its important message is that small stocks had *no* popular support from investors at the time, having seriously disappointed them over the prior twenty years ending in 1999. Investors' mind-sets at the time made it nearly impossible for them to buy small-cap stocks, much less buy them with enthusiasm. Anyone who understood the importance of mean reversion would have seen 1999 as a screaming buying opportunity, yet after the article's publication the response I received from investors was a big yawn. They were so focused on what had been working recently in the market—i.e., large-cap growth stocks—that they were blinded to the opportunity. As you try to make good investment decisions for the future, you will be confronted by this situation time and again. Say that by the time you read this, small stocks are in a short-term downtrend. I can virtually guarantee that you will be very tempted to ignore the long-term data and be more enticed by those stocks that have been performing well most recently. If so, you will be missing a wonderful opportunity, just as investors did in 1999.

Small-Cap Stocks Ascendant

The good news for long-term investors is that even with their recent strong performance, small-cap stocks are *still* a great opportunity. As we saw in figure 3–4, they are emerging from the largest performance gap from large-cap stocks in history. While large-cap stocks were recently dangerously above their long-term average, small-cap stocks are in the Promised Land—emerging from a twenty-year period in which their performance was one standard deviation *below* their long-term average.

TABLE 3–2 RETURNS AFTER EXTREME 20-YEAR REAL RETURNS

	Small Stocks Real 20-Year CAGR	
	7.48% or Lower	13.35% or Higher
Number of Occurrences	62	112
Minimum Return, 20 years later	11.76%	4.69%
Maximum Return, 20 years later	16.75%	12.15%
Average Return, 20 years later	14.03%	8.38%
Median Return, 20 years later	13.87%	8.43%
All Time High	17.91%	Jun-52
Current	10.38%	Dec-04
Implied Real Returns, 2022–2025	**7.62% to 9.62%**	

As I did with large stocks, I'll segregate the small-cap stocks by one standard deviation of return and look at the times when they were well above or below their long-term average, then examine their returns twenty years later. Over all rolling twenty-year periods, the average real annual compound return for small stocks is 10.42 percent. The standard deviation is 2.94 percent, so I'll look at the times when small stocks returned *less* than 7.48 percent and more than 13.35 percent over the previous twenty years. Table 3–2 and figures 3–5 and 3–6 summarize the results.

For the sixty-two overlapping rolling twenty-year periods when

FIGURE 3–5 REAL RETURN DISTRIBUTIONS 20 YEARS AFTER SMALL-CAP STOCK RETURNS ARE ONE STANDARD DEVIATION BELOW LONG-TERM AVERAGE

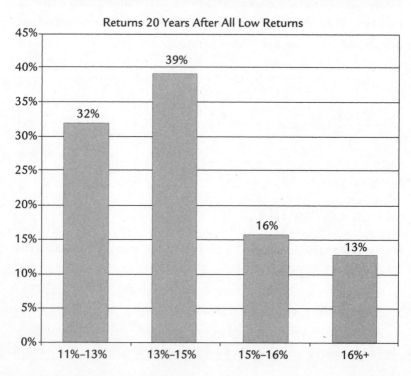

Returns 20 Years After All Low Returns

small stocks compounded at 7.48 percent or less, twenty years later the *minimum* return was 11.76 percent, the maximum 16.75 percent, and the average 14.03 percent. As figure 3–5 details, twenty years after turning in low returns for investors, small stocks returned more than 13 percent per year over the next twenty-year period *68 percent* of the time! And they *always* provided returns in excess of the twenty-year average after low return periods. Conversely, after the 112 times when they turned in returns much *higher* than their long-term average, the minimum return twenty years later was 4.69 percent; the maximum was 12.15 percent and the average 8.38 percent. Figure 3–6 shows that twenty years after great performance, returns from small stocks fell between 4 and 11 percent 98 percent of the time.

The good news is that as recently as March 2003, small stocks' returns were in the historically low range: their returns over the twenty years ending in March 2003 were 6.91 percent, more than one standard deviation below their long-term mean. This means that if they are to revert to their longer-term mean over the next twenty years, small stocks have an *excellent* chance of doing substantially better than large stocks. For now, I will take a conservative position and simply assume that they will deliver their historic 3.12 percent premium, plus a 1.50 percent premium to account for the fact that their recent twenty-year return was more than one standard deviation below their seventy-eight-year average.

My resulting forecast for small-cap stocks is an annual real rate of return between 7.6 and 9.6 percent over the next twenty years. If that doesn't sound particularly impressive, compare the terminal value of a twenty-year investment in large-cap stocks earning between 3 and 5 percent annually and small-cap stocks earning between 7.6 and 9.6 percent. If you invested $10,000 in large-cap stocks and earned 3 percent per year, your portfolio would be worth $18,061 in twenty years. If, however, you invested

FIGURE 3–6 REAL RETURN DISTRIBUTIONS 20 YEARS AFTER SMALL-CAP STOCK RETURNS ARE ONE STANDARD DEVIATION ABOVE LONG-TERM AVERAGE

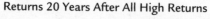

Returns 20 Years After All High Returns

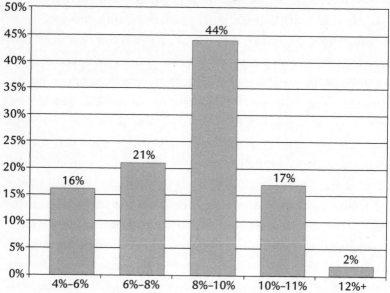

the same $10,000 in small-cap stocks and earned 7.6 percent a year, your $10,000 would grow to $43,437. If you earned the higher forecasted returns for each, the large-cap stocks would grow to $26,533 and the small-caps to $62,776. In chapters 8 and 9 I'll show you how to further enhance the performance of a small-cap portfolio. For now, keep in mind that all these return assumptions are quite conservative and approximate what I expect broad small-cap indexes like the Russell 2000 to compound in the years ahead.

New Methodology

It's important to note that I've changed my methodology since last publishing my research. In my previous books, I averaged the historical returns for the strategies I advocated, then simply assumed that you could earn similar returns into the future, provided your investment horizon was a long one. In light of this new work, my earlier approach appears naïve. I now feel it is better to look at how much better or worse any given investment performs in relationship to its benchmark, and then make forecasts based upon this difference. For example, I am projecting that the large-cap stocks that make up the S&P 500 will compound at 3 to 5 percent per year over the next twenty years, then add the 3 to 5 percent to the expected small-cap premium to forecast small-cap performance.

This method allows us to make forecasts that take current market dynamics into account, rather than simply assuming that we will be able to earn the average returns that we've seen over long periods in the past. After all, we've just lived through a tremendous bull market, and it would be foolish to assume that we can continue to generate double-digit returns in a far more trying market environment.

Chapter Three Highlights

◆ Small-cap stocks traditionally outperform large-cap stocks, with average returns 3.12 percent higher in any rolling twenty-year period.

◆ To maintain a neutral exposure to market capitalization, 25 percent of your portfolio should be invested in small- and mid-cap stocks and 75 percent should be in large-cap stocks. However, given my forecasts for large and small stocks over the next twenty years, this may not be an optimal allocation of assets.

◆ The small-cap premium is inversely proportional to the total returns generated by large-cap stocks. When large stocks
are doing particularly well, the small-cap premium is low to
negative, whereas when large stocks are doing poorly the
small-cap premium is above average. We are just now coming off the largest differential between the two in history.
Expect both to continue reverting to their long-term means.

◆ In the sixty-two periods in which small stocks did substantially worse than their long-term average, the average return
twenty years later was 14.03 percent and *all* returns were
higher than the long-term average. On March 31, 2003, small
stock returns were 6.91 percent per year for the prior twenty
years, one standard deviation *below* their long-term average.

◆ Our most conservative forecast for small stocks over the
next twenty years is 7.6 to 9.6 percent per year—nearly double that of large-cap stocks. We'll see in later chapters how
investors willing to use specific investment strategies within
the small-cap category can further enhance their expected
returns.

Note

To calculate his Small Stocks Index, Roger Ibbotson used multiple sources: For the period between 1926 and 1981, he used the
historical series developed by Professor Rolf W. Banz. This is composed of stocks making up the fifth quintile (i.e., the ninth and
tenth deciles) of the NYSE, which are the smallest 20 percent of
stocks by market capitalization. The portfolio was first formed
and ranked as of December 31, 1925, and held for five years, with
value weighted portfolio returns calculated monthly. Every five
years, the portfolio was rebalanced to again include stocks falling

in the ninth and tenth deciles by market capitalization. This process enabled Ibbotson to avoid survivorship bias by including the return after a delisting or failure of a stock. From 1982 to 2004, Ibbotson uses the Dimensional Fund Advisors (DFA) Small Company 9/10 Fund. The fund is a market value weighted index including the ninth and tenth deciles of the NYSE, plus stocks listed on the AMEX and OTC with similar market capitalizations. The fund's returns include transaction costs.

4

Showdown: Large-Cap Growth Versus Value

> The less a man knows about the past and the present the more insecure must be his judgment of the future.
>
> —Sigmund Freud

While we saw in the last chapter that the prospects for smaller stocks are much better than those for larger stocks, it would be imprudent to recommend that investors put all their money in small-cap stocks. The outright rejection of asset allocation was one of the gravest sins many investors committed during the bubble years. So, even though we can take solace in small-cap stocks' promising future, I would never invest my portfolio in one asset class or investment style. The market will inevitably face shorter periods of uncertainty over the next twenty years, where everything that might provide great returns over the long term is struggling in the shorter term. That's where good asset allocation comes in—ideally, your portfolio should be allocated so that something is always working.

Thus, our mission is to see which large-cap stocks we should invest in over the next twenty years. In this chapter, we'll look at the historical performance of large-cap stocks characterized by their *investment style*. In keeping with the theme of this book—that the twenty years ending in March 2000 were as close to a one-hundred-year flood in financial markets as any of us will see in our lifetimes—history will show us that large-cap growth stocks rarely serve up the performance that investors hope for. History has also shown that large-cap value stocks are a much better bet.

Growth Versus Value

Active investors are guided by styles, broadly called *growth* and *value*. Unlike indexes such as the S&P 500—which are traditionally style neutral but typically segregate stocks by market capitalization—style investors look beyond capitalization to the underlying characteristics of a stock. What type of stock they buy depends largely on their underlying philosophy.

Growth investors buy stocks that have higher-than-average growth in sales and earnings with expectations for more of the same. Growth investors believe in a company's potential and think a stock's price will follow its earnings and sales higher. Traditionally, growth stocks are characterized by investors' willingness to pay more for every dollar of current earnings, cash flow, or sales because they are betting that the company will increase them so rapidly that they will be rewarded handsomely over time. Thus, growth investors are most concerned with a company's *future*—and they're betting that it will be a bright one.

Value investors seek stocks with current market values substantially below true or liquidating value. They use factors like price-to-earnings ratios, price-to-sales ratios, and dividend yield to identify when a stock is selling below its intrinsic value. They bargain hunt, looking for stocks where they can buy a dollar's worth of assets for less than a dollar. Value investors believe in a company's balance sheet, thinking a stock's price will eventually rise to meet its intrinsic value. Unlike growth investors, value investors are deeply suspicious of rosy forecasts and prefer to judge a stock's value by *current* prevailing conditions. Therefore, they are unwilling to pay premiums for a stock's earnings, cash flow, or sales. They are far more likely to put their faith in stocks with low valuations and high dividend yields than those with great stories. Let's see who history proves right.

What Works on Wall Street Findings

In my book *What Works on Wall Street*, I analyzed fifty-two years of data for individual stocks using the S&P COMPUSTAT database, the largest, most extensive database of fundamental data available for U.S. stocks. The COMPUSTAT covers every stock traded in the United States, and the fifty-two years of available data cover every market environment except a great depression. What I found when looking at large-cap stocks was that all the value strategies I tested (in which investors purchased stocks with low PE ratios, price-to-book ratios, etc.) beat the market by substantial margins, and all the growth strategies (in which investors are willing to pay a premium for perceived higher growth rates) do considerably worse.

All of the large-cap growth strategies I tested were riskier than their value counterparts—and performed significantly worse. What's more, large-cap value strategies' performance was very consistent. All of the large-cap value strategies beat a universe of large stocks *at least* 86 percent of the time over all forty-three rolling ten-year periods I tested. All of the large-cap growth strategies, on the other hand, *failed* to beat the large stocks universe a majority of the time over all rolling ten-year periods. In short, I found that large-cap growth strategies consistently underperformed large-cap value strategies and were characterized by short, violent upsurges, generally when investors' expectations for the future were overly optimistic.

Looking Farther Back

Luckily, we can look even farther back in time by using data prepared by two academic economists, Eugene Fama and Ken French. Fama and French are pioneers in academic studies of stock market behavior, and created a series of style indexes in order to understand the long-term benefits of growth and value investing. Their data cover the market back to July 1927. (Details on how the Fama and French indexes are constructed and calculated can be found in the note at the end of this chapter.)

Figure 4–1 shows the growth of one dollar invested June 30, 1927, through December 31, 2004. Historically, large-cap value stocks have performed significantly better than both the S&P 500 and large-cap growth stocks. Between 1927 and 2004, an investment in large-cap value stocks did nearly six times as well as one in large-cap growth stocks and three times as well as an investment in the S&P 500. One dollar invested on June 30, 1927, in the Fama/French Large Value Index was worth $601 at the end of 2004, a real compound average annual return of 8.61 percent per year. The same dollar invested in the S&P 500 grew to $187 by the end of 2004, whereas one dollar invested in the Fama/French Large Growth Index grew to just $101, a real compound average

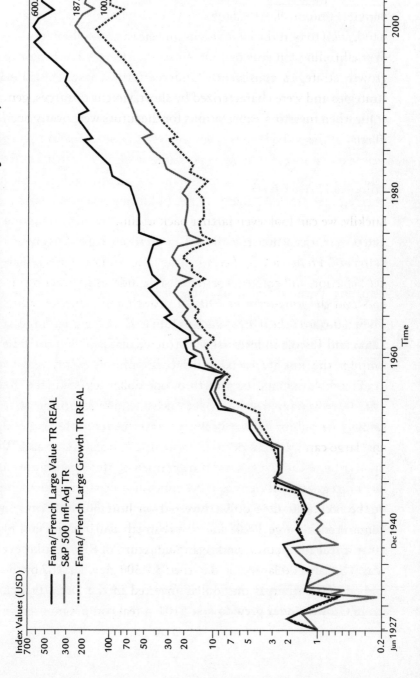

FIGURE 4-1 TERMINAL REAL VALUE OF $1 INVESTED JUNE 30, 1927

annual return of 6.13 percent, some 2.48 percent below an investment in the large value stocks.

It's also instructive to look at how the two schools of investing
perform when the market is stagnant. During the last prolonged
sideways market—the seventeen years between December 31, 1965,
and December 31, 1982—the S&P 500's real rate of return was zero.
One dollar invested on December 31, 1965, was worth exactly one
dollar at the end of 1982—seventeen years of *no real return!* Yet the
same dollar invested in large-cap value stocks was worth $2.26 at
the end of 1982, a real compound average annual return of 4.90
percent per year over that very disappointing seventeen years. So
who was the big loser over those seventeen years? Large-cap
growth stocks, where the one dollar fell to a value of 86 cents.

Rolling Twenty-Year Real Rates of Return

When we look at figures 4-2 through 4-4, we see that large-cap
value stocks consistently outperform both the S&P 500 and large-
cap growth stocks. For all overlapping rolling twenty-year real
rates of return, large-cap value stocks beat the S&P 500 in 638 of
the 691 overlapping twenty-year periods, or 92 percent of the
time. The minimum twenty-year real rate of return for large-cap
value stocks was 1.52 percent per year; the maximum was 17.01
percent and the average was a real return of 10.32 percent for all
rolling twenty-year periods. The worst large-cap value stocks ever
did compared to the S&P 500 was −1.21 percent for the twenty years
ending in February 2000. Their best comparative performance was
during the twenty years ending in August 1959, when they beat the
S&P 500 by 5.96 percent per year. On average, large-cap value
stocks outperformed the S&P 500 by 3.03 percent per year for all
rolling twenty-year periods.

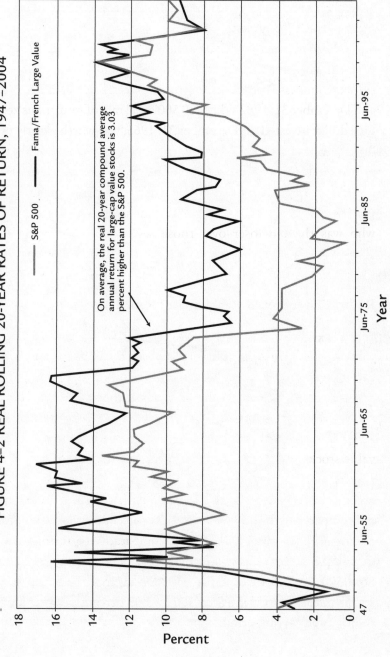

FIGURE 4–2 REAL ROLLING 20-YEAR RATES OF RETURN, 1947–2004

—— S&P 500   —— Fama/French Large Value

On average, the real 20-year compound average annual return for large-cap value stocks is 3.03 percent higher than the S&P 500.

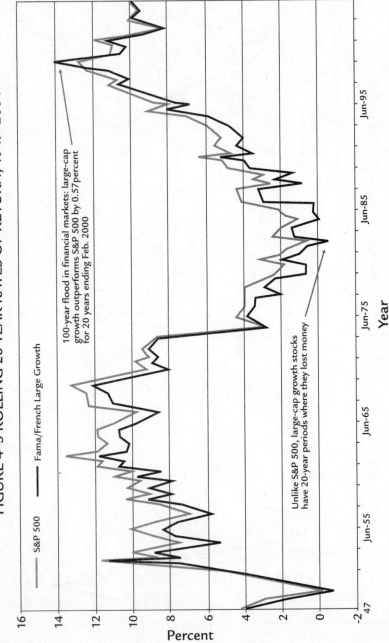

FIGURE 4-3 ROLLING 20-YEAR RATES OF RETURN, 1947–2004

S&P 500   Fama/French Large Growth

100-year flood in financial markets: large-cap growth outperforms S&P 500 by 0.57 percent for 20 years ending Feb. 2000

Unlike S&P 500, large-cap growth stocks have 20-year periods where they lost money

Year

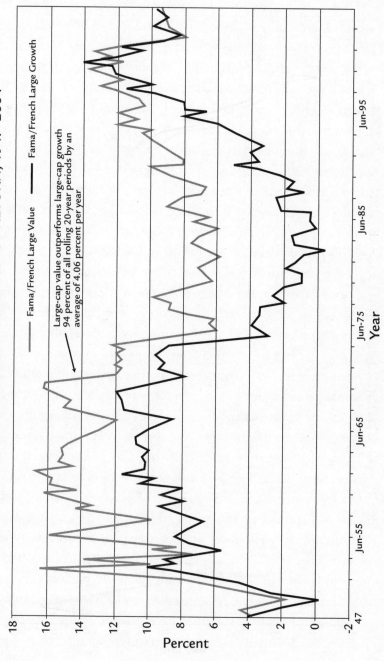

FIGURE 4-4 REAL ROLLING 20-YEAR RATES OF RETURN, 1947–2004

— Fama/French Large Value   — Fama/French Large Growth

Large-cap value outperforms large-cap growth 94 percent of all rolling 20-year periods by an average of 4.06 percent per year

When we compare the performance of large-cap value stocks against large-cap growth stocks, the news is even better—large-cap value beat large-cap growth in 651 of the 691 twenty-year periods, or 94 percent of the time. Indeed, the *only* twenty-year periods in which large-cap growth stocks beat large-cap value stocks were between 1999 and 2004, undoubtedly because of the influence of the Internet bubble. In *all* other rolling twenty-year periods, large-cap value stocks beat their growth competitors. Over all rolling twenty-year periods, the worst large-cap value stocks ever did was when they underperformed large-cap growth for the twenty years ending in February 2000 by −1.78 percent per year. On average, large-cap value stocks outperform large-cap growth stocks by 4.06 percent per year for any twenty-year rolling period.

Large-cap value stocks' long-term real rate of return over all twenty-year rolling periods is 10.32 percent. Looking at the performance of large-cap value stocks after they significantly over- or underperformed that 10.32 percent, we see that one standard deviation of return under the average would be returns of 6.91 percent or less over the previous twenty years, whereas one standard deviation above would be returns of 13.74 percent or more over the previous twenty years. Table 4–1 shows the results after large-cap value stocks have extreme twenty-year rates of return. In all instances where they earned less than 6.91 percent over the previous twenty years, their performance over the subsequent twenty years was quite strong, averaging 12.77 percent per year. Indeed, figure 4–5 shows that in periods after large-cap value stocks had lackluster twenty-year returns, 67 percent of all future twenty-year returns were in excess of 12 percent and the largest concentration of returns (44 percent) were between 12 and 15 percent per year.

Conversely, when large-cap value stocks have turned in outstanding returns over the prior twenty years, the results twenty years hence are more modest—most returns fall in the 5 to 7 per-

TABLE 4–1 RETURNS AFTER EXTREME
20-YEAR REAL RETURNS

	Large-Cap Value Real 20-Year CAGR	
	6.91% or Lower	13.74% or Higher
Number of Occurrences	98	129
Minimum Return, 20 years later	8.78%	5.61%
Maximum Return, 20 years later	16.49%	12.06%
Average Return, 20 years later	12.77%	7.17%
Median Return, 20 years later	12.58%	6.96%
All Time High	17.01%	Mar-62
Current	9.28%	Dec-04
Implied Real Return, 2022–2025	**6.03% to 8.03%**	

FIGURE 4–5 20-YEAR REAL RETURNS FOR LARGE-CAP
VALUE AFTER ALL LOW RETURNS, 1947–2004

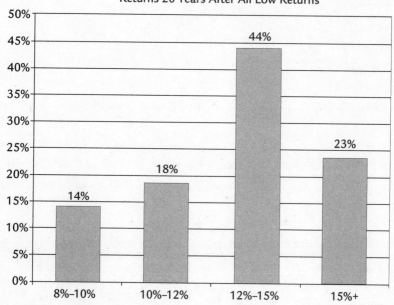

Returns 20 Years After All Low Returns

cent range, and on average, they provide investors with returns of 7.17 percent per year even *after* twenty years of outstanding performance. Figure 4–6 illustrates the distribution of these large-cap value returns.

Large-Cap Value Premium

Large-cap value stocks so consistently beat both the S&P 500 and large-cap growth stocks that a historical premium emerges—an average of 3.03 percent per year above the S&P 500 and 4.06 percent per year over large-cap growth stocks. Figure 4–7 shows the rolling twenty-year real premium earned by large-cap value stocks against the S&P 500.

FIGURE 4–6 20-YEAR REAL RETURNS FOR LARGE-CAP VALUE AFTER ALL HIGH RETURNS, 1947–2004

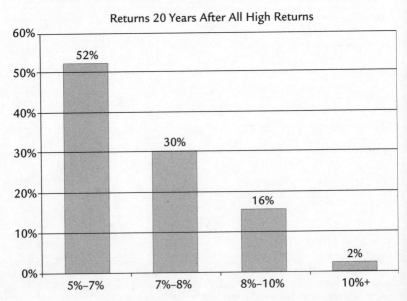

Returns 20 Years After All High Returns

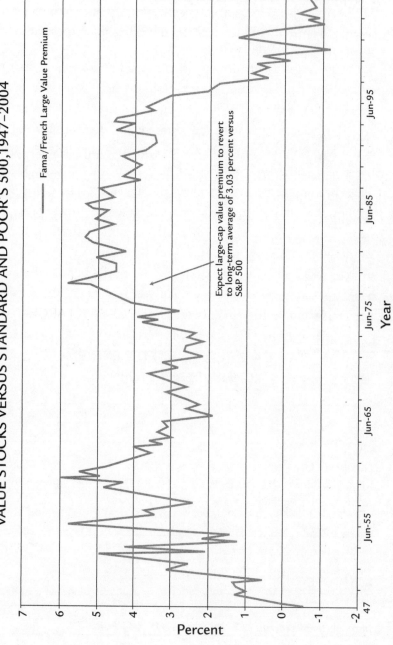

VALUE STOCKS VERSUS STANDARD AND POOR'S 500, 1947–2004

— Fama/French Large Value Premium

Expect large-cap value premium to revert to long-term average of 3.03 percent versus S&P 500

Year

Percent

Disappointing Large Growth Returns

Figure 4–3 and table 4–2 show the results for large-cap growth stocks over all rolling twenty-year periods. When compared to the S&P 500, large-cap growth stocks consistently offer lower returns over all overlapping twenty-year periods, with the exception of the twenty years at the end of the bubble in February 2000. Large-cap growth stocks' real twenty-year returns are truly pathetic—beating the S&P 500 in just 21 of all 691 overlapping periods— or just 3 percent of the time. And the few times they did manage to beat the S&P 500 they did so by minuscule margins; on average a measly 0.11 percent.

For all rolling twenty-year periods, large-cap growth stock returns ranged from a minimum of –0.52 percent per year (the first twenty-year loss we've seen in any of the equity categories), to a high of 14.17 percent per year at the end of the bubble. On average, large-cap growth stocks earned real returns of 6.26 percent per year over all rolling twenty-year periods.

TABLE 4–2 RETURNS AFTER EXTREME 20-YEAR REAL RETURNS

	Large-Cap Growth Real 20-Year CAGR	
	2.43% or Lower	10.09% or Higher
Number of Occurrences	113	71
Minimum Return, 20 years later	8.12%	–0.52%
Maximum Return, 20 years later	14.17%	3.27%
Average Return, 20 years later	10.89%	1.20%
Median Return, 20 years later	11.04%	1.19%
All Time High	14.17%	Mar-00
Current	9.83%	Dec-04
Implied Real Return, 2022–2025	**1.97% to 3.97%**	

When we look at the returns of large-cap growth stocks after they were one standard deviation above or below their long-tem average of 6.26 percent, we find that even after turning in returns of 2.43 percent or less for the previous twenty years, the subsequent twenty-year returns aren't very exciting. After historically low twenty-year returns, the large-cap growth returns twenty years later ranged from 8.12 percent to 14.17 percent, with an average of 10.89 percent; on average, slightly less than the S&P 500. Figure 4–8 shows us that 78 percent of these returns were between 8 and 11 percent. Thus, even after a punishing twenty-year return, large-cap growth stocks offer little better than S&P 500–like returns in the coming 20 years.

More germane to current conditions, however, is how large-cap growth stocks performed twenty years after better than average

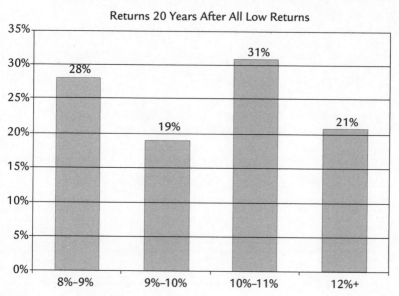

FIGURE 4–8 20-YEAR REAL RETURNS FOR LARGE-CAP GROWTH AFTER ALL LOW RETURNS, 1947–2004

Returns 20 Years After All Low Returns

twenty-year real returns. Large-cap growth stocks marked their best twenty-year return *ever* on March 31, 2000, when they returned 14.17 percent over the prior twenty years. Table 4–2 and figure 4–9 show the results of an investment in large-cap growth stocks after unusually high twenty-year returns—in the subsequent twenty years large-cap growth stocks are horrific investments. For the seventy-one periods in which large-cap growth stocks marked twenty-year rates of return of 10.09 percent or better, twenty years later the worst return was −0.52 percent; the best was a gain of 3.27 percent and the average return was 1.20 percent! Figure 4–9 shows us that 73 percent of these returns fell between −1 and 2

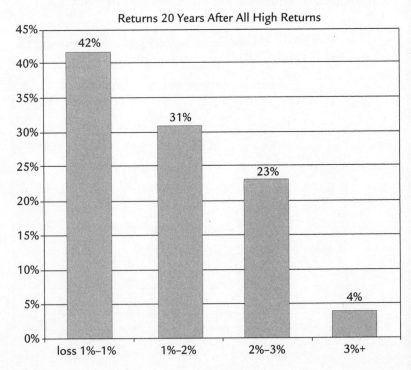

FIGURE 4–9 20-YEAR REAL RETURNS FOR LARGE-CAP GROWTH AFTER ALL HIGH RETURNS, 1947–2004

percent per year! These returns are hardly encouraging for growth stocks' prospects in the coming twenty years.

Why Value Beats Growth

Valuation matters. It really is as simple as that. There's a good reason they call economics the dismal science—the rules of economics are ruthless and cruel and care little for people's hopes and expectations. That is at the heart of why value stocks so consistently beat growth stocks. Over time, the rules of economics insist that only *real* profits and dividends are rewarded. When you act as a value investor and consistently pay less and get more, you wind up doing much better than those willing to pay more and get less.

Growth investors are generally willing to pay huge premiums because they get seduced by the prospects of some "outstanding" stock with a great story. The simple truth is that investor sentiment drives growth stock prices. The more enthusiastic investors and analysts are about the prospects for growth, the more they are willing to pay. As we'll see in chapter 6, investors who get caught up in this kind of sentiment are using the irrational part of their brains, the part having to do with emotion and love. And while those are great parts of the brain to engage when you are searching for a mate, they wreak havoc when put in charge of investment decisions.

I reprinted part of my article on Internet valuations in chapter 1, but the second part of that story was a look at two of the Internet bubble darlings, AOL and Amazon.com. Here's what I said about them in 1999:

> *A great company is not always a great investment. Take Amazon.com. It has a market-cap greater than the dollar value of all the books sold in this country, yet the company has never*

made money and boasts a negative profit margin of 20.4%. And more of the same is forecasted for years into the future!

I love Amazon's Web site, yet recently discovered that it's cheaper for me to buy the paperback version of my book How to Retire Rich *at my local Barnes & Noble or Borders! At Amazon, with the shipping and handling, I've got to shell out $14.35 for a $13.00 book. Even after 6% state sales tax, I'm still better off at my local bookstore than Amazon.*

So, what about other books, like What Works on Wall Street *or Tom Wolfe's* A Man in Full? *For* What Works, *Amazon saves me eight cents off the list price (after shipping), but almost $5.00 for* A Man in Full. *Looks good, I'll buy, right? Wrong. Unlike a regular store, where I'm physically present and disinclined to run all over town looking for a better bargain, I have no such limitations on the Web. In Cyberspace, there is no salesperson to feel indebted to—just a better bargain to be found.*

In Cyberspace, I don't feel indebted to any salesperson or shop owner: I'm just looking for the best deal. In Cyberspace, I'll take a minute and pop over to Bestbookbuys.com, where I find that I can buy A Man in Full *from Booksamillion.com for $19.58— about $5.00 less than Amazon.com charges. And since I can buy the book in the same amount of time—you know where I'll buy it.*

Amazon's business model depends upon their ability to charge premium prices for commodity products like books, CDs and pharmaceuticals, just because people like the shopping experience at Amazon. But the rub is that in Cyberspace, the experience is pretty much the same no matter where you buy your commodity product. Like my friend Dave Chilton, author of The Wealthy Barber, *says, "when I go to a fine restaurant to enjoy the ambience, the deal is that I've got to eat their food. The same is not true on the Internet. I can go to Amazon, read the reviews and make maximum use of their site's ambience, then in ten* seconds click over to www.acses.com or www.bestbookbuys.com and find the lowest price, which is almost never from Amazon."

And what's going to happen when a bricks and mortar company like Wal-Mart—with real earnings and sustainable margins—decides to get into the game? What if they finally find a business model that shows it can turn a profit on the web, and they put up a site called Bestprice.com, guaranteeing everything sold there will have the lowest price anywhere, or double your money back? Imagine convenience married to price, all backed by a well-known company with a real operating history. Amazon.com may be a great story now—but I think a few years from now the story of the rise and fall of its price will be even more riveting.

One-Sixth of the World's Population? No Problem!

Even when Internet companies have real earnings, the dot com mania is sending valuations into the stratosphere. America Online trades at 635 time trailing earnings, yet has a negative Economic Value Added (EVA) of 10.3%. That means that investors are betting its entire $130 billion market-cap depends on future growth. To just maintain current valuations, AOL will have to get one-sixth of the world's population to pay full price for its service, and do that every year!

Jeremy Siegel points out in the Wall Street Journal: "AOL is currently selling at more than 700 times its earnings for the past 12 months and 450 times its expected 1999 earnings. These are unprecedented valuations for a firm with this market value. . . . If AOL in its 'maturity' sports a PE ratio of 30—and this is a ratio that still anticipates substantial growth—it will have to generate net profits of about $6.7 billion per year to maintain a $200 billion market value. In 1998 General Electric was the only American firm with profits that high."

Since the article's publication in 1999, Amazon's share price plummeted from $85 to $6 in 2001 and AOL ceased to be an independent company—after its merger with Time Warner the combined entity's price fell from $76 to $12 in 2003.

Hindsight now makes it clear to us that these stocks were drastically overvalued. Back in 1999, however, my opinions garnered mostly derision and ridicule; people thought I was a bit of a fuddy-duddy who just "didn't get it." Back in the day, Amazon and AOL were the shining beacons of the new Internet economy, and that's where growth investors get most tripped up. They became utterly seduced by the possibilities of a new industry. And do you know what? They *always have!* The Internet madness is the freshest in our collective memory, but it is just one example of the same old story.

It's the Story, Stupid!

People loved Amazon.com and AOL for their sexy and compelling stories. That is why otherwise intelligent investors will pay so much and throw caution to the wind—they get seduced and caught up in a great story. *Every* era has its sexy growth stories—in the nineteenth century, it was railroads and telegraphs; in the 1920s automobile companies, radio companies, and motion pictures; in the 1950s aluminum and atomic energy; in the 1970s energy and mining stocks; in the 1980s and early 1990s computer makers and biotech concerns; in the late 1990s, the Internet and anything having to do with Silicon Valley. Tomorrow it might be nanotechnology and security stocks. The point is, there will *always* be a new story to ignite growth investors' imaginations and the rules of economics will *always* crush those valuations after investors have taken them to unreasonable heights. When investors buy hot stocks with extreme valuations, they often end up paying one hundred times or more for each dollar of a company's sales or earnings. Hope springs eternal in these investors' hearts: they're betting the company will expand so quickly that their investment proves worthwhile. Yet the vital link to this outlandish behavior is the *story*. It's the story that ignites our imaginations and emotions; it's the story that we cling to when trying to justify an investment. We personalize our love for the great story stocks we buy, thinking of them as "our company."

I've tested this theory by stripping the name and story from a stock, then showing people the underlying numbers. When you do this, people act rationally and *refuse* to pay an outlandish price for a stock. If I asked you to buy my store on the corner, but told you that you had to pay me $1,000 for every dollar of my sales, you'd say I was crazy. But slap a sexy name and concept on it—say Cybercash, which had a hot story about how it was going to make the Internet a safe place to transact business—and investors gladly paid two thousand times sales! The power of a good story is unbelievably enticing—but it is a terribly dangerous siren song. Investors who pay ridiculous sums for a sexy stock will live to regret their folly.

Here's a little exercise to further illustrate my point. Stop for a moment and ask yourself: Which of the following two groups of stocks would you rather own? The first includes Google, the undisputed king of search engines on the Internet; MedImmune, Inc., a biotechnology company focusing on infectious diseases, oncology, and immunology; Equity Residential (EQR), an integrated real estate company engaged in the acquisition, development, ownership, management, and operation of multifamily properties; and Computer Associates International, Inc., a provider of management software.

The second group consists of POSCO, a Korean firm that manufactures and sells a line of steel products, including hot-rolled and cold-rolled products, plates, wire rods, silicon steel sheets, and

stainless steel products; PG&E Corporation, an energy-based holding company that conducts its business through Pacific Gas and
Electric Company, a public utility operating in northern and central California; Sears, Roebuck and Co. (Sears), a multiline retailer
that offers a wide array of merchandise and related services and is
among the largest retailers in North America; and Bank Bradesco
S.A., a private-sector bank that provides a range of banking and
financial products and services in Brazil.

Chances are you instinctively went for the first group, yet each
of those names currently has a PE ratio exceeding 100 and belongs squarely in the large-cap growth category, whereas each of
the second group has a PE of 5 or lower and belongs to the large-
cap value group that has trounced large-cap growth so thoroughly
over time. Discussing Google's search engine technology may win
you attention at a cocktail party, but holding forth on the merits
of POSCO's cold-rolled steel products is going to send the gang
around the office water cooler scampering back to their cubicles.
The simple truth is that large-cap growth stocks are almost always
more interesting to talk about, but that does not make them good
investments. At the end of the day, the simple and straightforward rules of economics matter—they always have in the past, and
they always will in the future.

We would have seen a similar story back in the early part of
the twentieth century with car manufacturers. According to economist Lester Thurow, between 1900 and 1920, over two thousand
companies were formed to make automobiles! By the late teens
and early 1920s, this number was whittled down to a few dozen
firms. Talk about a *huge* failure rate. The dozens of automobile
companies of the era were the growth stocks of the decade, yet
fewer than ten years later, another 80 percent of them were out of
business and the industry was dominated by just three companies! All of the excited investors of the 1920s were bitterly disap-

pointed with the lack of performance they got from the hot growth sector that defined the automakers.

Value Stocks Are Boring

Face it—value stocks are dreadfully boring! Growth stocks are sexy, cool, and play to people's hopes for what the world can become. They almost always represent brand-new industries that ignite investors' imaginations and their dreams of unlimited possibilities. In chapter 6 we'll also see that large growth stocks' prices are driven by overly optimistic estimates for future growth, which in turn dovetails with many investors' propensity to overconfidence and optimism about the future. The truth is that all of us want to be perceived as forward-looking and dynamic. All of us, despite our age, want to feel hip and part of the in-crowd that "gets it." No one wants to be sidelined or labeled a Luddite. Yet it is exactly that kind of sentiment that drives growth stocks to unsustainable levels—investors literally price them to perfection. The problem is, rarely is there any such thing as perfection, especially when it comes to investing.

Value Stocks Are More Rationally Priced

Thus do value stocks end up doing better than growth over almost all rolling twenty-year periods—they typify stocks where expectations are very *low* as opposed to growth stocks where expectations are very *high*. Investors focus on stocks like Microsoft, forgetting that as it gets larger and larger, it has a harder and harder time delivering outsized results. As a company gets bigger and bigger, the laws of mathematics take over and make it nearly impossible for that company to continue delivering huge gains year after year. Yet it seems to take investors an inordinate amount of time to figure this out—remember, people willingly bought AOL at 635 times earnings!

With value stocks, you're often paying less than average for stocks with solid—if dull—earnings and dividends. By doing so, you're putting the laws of economics on your side. Will some of your stocks fail to live up to expectations? Of course, but since you didn't pay too much for them to begin with, you'll probably avoid the terrifying plunges that overpriced growth stocks frequently deliver.

You get the picture—in the long run, value consistently beats growth because it is based on *real* earnings and dividend yields, not fantastic stories. Remember that the next time you see someone on CNBC touting the latest and greatest breakthrough stock—chances are, it's more likely to break down than break through.

Large-Cap Growth and Value's Twenty-Year Outlook

Over all twenty-year periods, large-cap value stocks almost always outperform both the S&P 500 and large-cap growth stocks. Currently, the twenty-year rate of return for large-cap value stocks is below its historical average. It's not a full standard deviation below, however, so I will base my forecast on the traditional large-cap value premium of 3.03 percent over the S&P 500. Adding this premium to our forecast for the S&P 500 (between 3 and 5 percent annually over the next twenty years), I arrive at an expected rate of return for large-cap value stocks between 6.03 and 8.03 percent through 2022–2025. In chapter 8, I'll focus on stock selection strategies that improve on this forecast.

Large-cap growth stocks, on the other hand, are coming off their best twenty-year performance ever. History tells us to expect rather meager real annual returns between −1 and +3 percent over the next twenty years. Subtracting the amount that large-cap growth traditionally lags the S&P 500 (a little more than 1 percent for all rolling twenty-year periods), I expect that large-cap growth stocks will only return 1.97 to 3.97 percent for the period through 2022–2025. Note that there are subperiods in which large-cap growth names do very well, so even with this anemic long-term forecast, I do include large-cap growth stocks in my recommended portfolio allocations. The key is what types of growth stocks you should buy. There are many ways to guard against overvaluation. I will discuss this and recommend overall asset allocation strategies in chapter 11.

Chapter Four Highlights

◆ Large-cap value stocks traditionally beat both the S&P 500 and large-cap growth stocks over all rolling twenty-year periods. We are emerging from a highly anomalous period that ended on March 31, 2000, where large-cap value underperformed both the S&P 500 and large-cap growth stocks. Expect them to do significantly better than both groups over the next twenty years. The forecast for large-cap value stocks over that period is an annual real rate of return between 6.03 and 8.03 percent.

◆ Large-cap growth stocks traditionally underperform the S&P 500 and large-cap value stocks. They are coming off their best twenty-year real rate of return *ever*. In all other instances when large-cap growth stocks have significantly outperformed their long-term average, they went on to perform horribly over the ensuing twenty-year period. Expect large-cap growth stocks to underperform both the S&P 500 and large-cap value stocks over the next twenty years. The forecast for large-cap growth over the period is an annual real rate of return between 1.97 and 3.97 percent.

◆ Large-cap growth stocks underperform because investors, intoxicated by overly optimistic estimates for huge earnings growth, push prices to extremely high valuations which prove unsustainable when the forecasted growth fails to materialize or is not sustained. Later we will examine ways to select growth stocks that do not suffer from these extreme valuations.

◆ Large-cap value stocks outperform because they tend to have low valuations and higher dividend yields. We'll see later how this combination leads to an excellent method for selecting outstanding large-cap value stocks.

◆ Stories are just that—stories. Value investors rely less on hope and hype and more on factual evidence like current valuation. Over time, this leads to returns that far exceed those of the "new-new thing."

Note

To create their indexes, Fama and French use all stocks traded on the New York Stock Exchange to set both growth and value break points. They then applied these break points to all stocks traded on the New York Stock Exchange, the American Stock Exchange, and NASDAQ to construct each index. Portfolios are formed at the end of June of each year, and then held to the end of June of the following year, when they are rebalanced. To determine if a stock should be placed in the value or growth group, Fama and French use the book value of equity divided by market capitalization. Value companies will have a *high* book-to-market ratio, while growth companies will have a *low* book-to-market ratio. I then adjust their returns for inflation to arrive at a real rate of return. Fama and French's findings are very similar to the results of my research in *What Works on Wall Street*. I am therefore confident in the validity of their data, which goes back to 1927. (My research on the S&P COMPUSTAT database goes back to 1952.)

5

Which Bonds Are Right for My Portfolio?

Treasuries provide not risk-free return but "return-free risk."

—*Grant's Interest Rate Observer*

Bonds are much different from stocks. They have a more straightforward relationship between price and yield than that of stocks, and are far more sensitive to the effects of inflation. With bonds, price and yield are inversely proportional—every time yields go *up*, bond prices go *down*; every time yields go *down*, bond prices go *up*. The magnitude of the price increase and decrease is contingent on the duration of the bond: the longer the bond has until it matures, the greater the magnitude of its price movement when interest rates rise or fall.

Thus, long-term bonds will earn the greatest gains when interest rates are falling and shorter-term bonds will earn the least. Bonds come in all duration periods, from one year to thirty years and beyond. There are as many types of bonds as there are durations—the safest bonds (i.e., with the lowest risk) are issued by the U.S. government and the largest U.S. corporations. Traditionally, corporate bonds offer higher yields because they have an implicit default risk, which is based on investors' assumptions about the company's ability to repay its debt. Companies with excellent creditworthiness have bonds that are ranked from A to AAA by Moody's or Standard and Poor's. Bonds issued by companies that the rating services believe are less likely to be able to repay them are called *junk bonds,* and have gained in popularity over the last two decades. Junk bonds traditionally pay much higher yields as a consequence of their shaky credit ratings, but they are also the most likely to default on their obligations, leaving the bondholder feeling more like a bag holder.

In this chapter we will be looking specifically at U.S. Treasury bonds and bills, as they offer the closest thing to "riskless" returns that fixed income securities have to offer. We'll see that the prospects for U.S. Treasuries will be applicable to all bonds or bond funds that you might consider adding to your portfolio. I'll use a methodology similar to the one used for stocks—first I'll review the real returns that bonds and T-bills have earned historically, then analyze the returns over rolling twenty-year periods.

Ibbotson defines long-term bonds as those U.S. Treasury bonds with durations of twenty years or more. Intermediate-term bonds—the shortest duration noncallable bonds—have maturities not less than five years, and U.S. T-bills are thirty days in duration. As always, we will only look at real, inflation-adjusted rates of return.

Bonds Offer Modest Returns

The results are fairly horrific—unless you were lucky enough to load up on bonds in September 1981, when interest rates were at their highest levels in U.S. history. Over time, your chances of earning a *negative* real twenty-year rate of return from long-term U.S. bonds were better than fifty-fifty! Figure 5–1 and table 5–1 show that one dollar invested in 1927 grew to just $5.40 if invested in long-term U.S. bonds, a compound return of 2.2 percent over the seventy-eight years. Investors in U.S. intermediate-term bonds earned virtually the same amount—one dollar invested in 1927 grew to $5.32, a real compound return of 2.18 percent. (This is *extremely* important, as we'll see in a few pages.) Investors in T-bills barely managed to stay ahead of inflation—one dollar invested in 1927 grew to just $1.57 at the end of 2004, a real average annual compound return of just 0.59 percent.

Fifty-three Years Under Water

The real rate of return for long-term bonds and T-bills is directly tied to inflation and regulations that enforced an interest rate ceiling on banks after the Depression. An investor buying long-term bonds or U.S. T-bills in 1931 would have had to wait more than

TABLE 5–1 REAL RETURNS FOR FIXED-INCOME SECURITIES, JUNE 30, 1927–DECEMBER 31, 2004

	Geometric Mean (%)	$1 Becomes:
U.S. LT Gvt Infl-Adj TR	2.2	$5.39
U.S. IT Gvt Infl-Adj TR	2.18	$5.32
U.S. 30 Day T-Bill Infl-Adj TR	0.59	$1.57

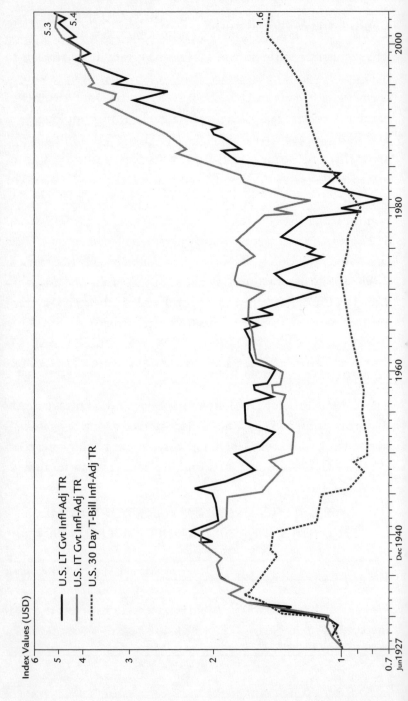

FIGURE 5–1 TERMINAL REAL RETURN VALUE OF $1 INVESTED IN 1927

TABLE 5–2 REAL RETURNS FOR FIXED-INCOME INSTRUMENTS OVER 53 YEARS, DECEMBER 31, 1931–DECEMBER 31, 1984

	Geometric Mean (%)	Ending Index Value	Maximum Decline (%) During Period
U.S. LT Gvt Infl-Adj TR	−0.06	$0.97	−67.24
U.S. IT Gvt Infl-Adj TR	0.66	$1.42	−43.6
U.S. 30 Day T-Bill Infl-Adj TR	−0.41	$0.81	−48.76

fifty-three years for his investment to make any money at all! Table 5-2 shows the real returns for bonds and bills between 1931 and 1984, and shows that anyone investing one dollar in long-term U.S. Treasuries *lost* three cents on the value of their dollar investment over the fifty-three years, whereas someone investing in T-bills saw their dollar shrink to just 81 cents! Only those who invested in intermediate-term bonds over the period made money.

The irony is that investors view U.S. bonds and bills as the *safest* investment they can make! History shows us that this is completely false. Imagine the exodus from stocks if they had fifty-three-year periods where they lost money—it would be virtually impossible to get *anyone* to invest in the stock market. What's more, the twenty-year rolling analysis shows that for a *majority* of the rolling twenty-year periods, investors in long-term U.S. bonds lost money!

Rolling Twenty-Year Periods

Figure 5-2 shows the rolling twenty-year real rates of return for an investment in long-term U.S. bonds. The best they ever did was a gain of 9.38 percent for the twenty years ending September 2001;

the worst was a loss of 3.12 percent for the twenty years ending September 1981. The average twenty-year return for long-term U.S. bonds was a paltry gain of 0.97 percent over all twenty-year periods between 1947 and 2004. Long-term bonds provided investors with negative returns in 402 of the 691 rolling twenty-year periods, or *58 percent of the time!* Looking at figure 5–2, we see that the real twenty-year rate of return for long-term U.S. bonds went negative in the early 1950s and stayed under water until 1986! Truly a horrible performance for an instrument viewed as the "safest" investment for conservative investors.

Figures 5–2 and 5–3 also show us that it wasn't just equity markets that experienced a perfect storm—bonds also saw the best returns that any of us are likely to see again in our lifetimes. In September 1981, the U.S. economy was reeling—runaway inflation and unemployment were destroying its core. Popular movies and books of the era depicted a world in which the United States would lose its economic supremacy to the Japanese as our industrial core decayed. Between 1978 and 1980, OPEC doubled the price of oil, pushing the United States and other industrial countries into the deepest recession since the Depression of the 1930s. U.S. unemployment was above 10 percent, higher than at any time since the 1940s. The nominal yield on long-term bonds topped 14 percent and investor sentiment was nearly as bleak as it had been during the depression. It was truly an act of faith to buy long-term bonds—but investors who did so were richly rewarded over the next twenty years. The U.S. government, particularly the Federal Reserve, finally got its act together. First under the leadership of Paul Volcker and then Alan Greenspan, the Fed broke the back of inflation with a lot of help from "bond market vigilantes" who, after the repeal of regulation Q, a Depression-era law that enforced a ceiling on interest rates, were quite willing to push interest rates to any height to ensure that they would receive a decent real rate of return.

FIGURE 5-2 REAL ROLLING 20-YEAR RATES OF RETURNS, 1947–2004

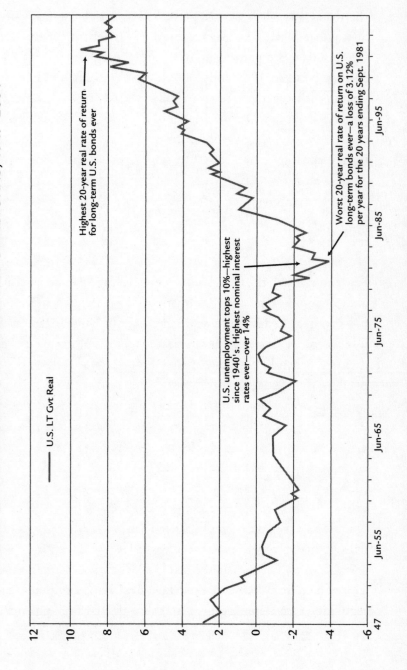

— U.S. LT Gvt Real

Highest 20-year real rate of return for long-term U.S. bonds ever

U.S. unemployment tops 10%—highest since 1940's. Highest nominal interest rates ever—over 14%

Worst 20-year real rate of return on U.S. long-term bonds ever—a loss of 3.12% per year for the 20 years ending Sept. 1981

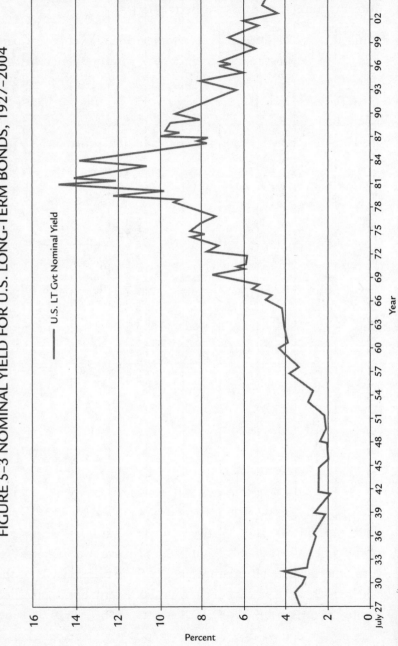

FIGURE 5–3 NOMINAL YIELD FOR U.S. LONG-TERM BONDS, 1927–2004

Intermediate-Term Bonds a Better Bet

While intermediate-term bonds also have many twenty-year periods where they lost money, their odds of making money are considerably higher than those of long-term bonds. Figure 5–4 shows
the rolling real twenty-year rate of returns for intermediate-term
bonds between 1947 and 2004. The best twenty-year return intermediate-term bonds earned was a real annual return of 6.98 percent for the twenty years ending September 2001; their worst was
a loss of 2.13 percent for the twenty years ending December 1959.
The average real return for all rolling twenty-year periods was a
gain of 1.32 percent.

Unlike long-term bonds, intermediate-term bonds only served
up twenty-year losses to investors in 206 of the 691 rolling twenty-
year periods, or 30 percent of the time. What's more, intermediate-
term bonds had much lower volatility than long-term bonds
while providing virtually the same long-term return and much
higher returns over all twenty-year holding periods. In the 691
rolling twenty-year periods, intermediate-term bonds outperform
long-term bonds 57 percent of the time. They also have a *lower*
correlation to stocks than long-term bonds—the correlation of
long-term bonds with the S&P 500 between June 30, 1927, and
December 31, 2004, was 0.16, whereas it was 0.14 for intermediate-
term bonds. That means intermediate-term bonds are more likely
to provide positive returns when stock prices are declining—
analyzing all 919 rolling twelve-month periods between 1927 and
2004, the S&P 500 had negative returns 300 times, or 33 percent
of the time. When the S&P 500 had a negative twelve-month return, intermediate-term bonds had *positive* returns in 173 of the
300 periods, or 58 percent of the time. Long-term bonds provided
positive returns in 157 of the 300 periods, or 52 percent of the time.

Finally, when interest rates are rising, intermediate-term bonds

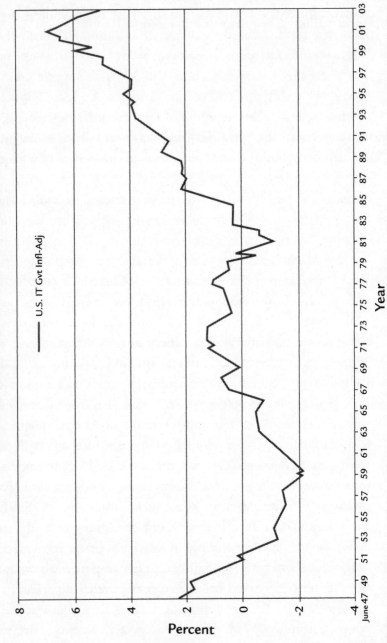

FIGURE 5-4 REAL ROLLING 20-YEAR RATES OF RETURN FOR U.S. INTERMEDIATE-TERM BONDS, 1947–2004

are much better performers, since they have much shorter durations and are therefore less subject to duration risk than their longer-term counterparts.

U.S. Treasury Bills

Finally, we will look at the returns from short-term U.S. Treasury bills, which can also be used as proxies for money market funds. Figure 5–4 shows the real returns for all rolling twenty-year periods between 1947 and 2004. The best returns from T-bills were a gain of 2.95 percent per year for the twenty years ending December 2000; the worst returns were a loss of 3.20 percent per year for the twenty years ending April 1952. The average real twenty-year return from T-bills was an anemic 0.13 percent per year over all rolling twenty-year periods.

The loss of 3.2 percent per year for the period between 1932 and 1952 shows that investors cannot rely on T-bills to keep up with inflation. Indeed, in 234 of the 691 rolling twenty-year periods analyzed, T-bills had negative returns. That's more than one-third of all the twenty-year periods analyzed, and a reminder that "safe" investments can often be anything but. The greatest irony of all is that T-bills show us that making timid choices with our investments can leave us with a portfolio whose purchasing power becomes seriously degraded over time. Clearly, investors need to re-think what is truly risky and what is not. In my opinion, the gravest risk investors face is not short-term volatility but long-term degradation of their purchasing power. Thus, investors must understand that investing in T-bills will at *best* keep them about even with inflation. At worst it will rob them of purchasing power.

Treasury Inflation Protected Securities (TIPS)

We now have a new weapon in our arsenal to use when attempting to forecast the expected real rate of returns of bonds over the next twenty years—inflation protected bonds. Issued for the first time by the U.S. Treasury in 1997, they have gained in popularity over the years. Here's how the U.S. Treasury's Web site describes them:

> TIPS provide investors with an investment option that protects against the effects of inflation. Like all marketable US Treasury securities, TIPS are backed by the full faith and credit of the US Government. TIPS are available to individual and institutional investors alike.
>
> Interest payments on TIPS are made semi-annually and are linked to the Consumer Price Index for Urban Consumers (CPI-U). The underlying value of the principal grows at the same rate that prices (as measured by CPI-U) rise. When the principal grows, interest payments grow also since interest payments are a fixed percentage of principal. At maturity, if inflation has occurred and increased the value of the underlying security, Treasury pays the owner the higher inflation-adjusted principal. If, however, deflation has occurred and decreased the value of the underlying security, the investor receives the original face value of the security.
>
> Earnings from TIPS are exempt from state and local income taxes just as other US Treasury notes and bonds. TIPS owners pay federal income tax on interest payments in the year they are received and on growth in principal in the year that it occurs.

Thus, the current yield of a ten- or twenty-year TIPS will give you the *exact* expected rate of return for each duration series *if you hold them to maturity*. Their day-to-day prices will still fluctuate like other bonds, but if you hold them for their entire duration, you are assured of what your real rate of return will be when the bond matures. As I write this in May of 2005, the ten-year TIPS bond has a yield of 1.57 percent and the twenty-year TIPS a yield of 1.70 percent, making those our effective expected rate of return for bonds for the period ending 2022–2025.

TIPS Are Not Perfect

While the current yields of inflation-protected bonds serve as an ideal proxy for forecasting the long-term expected rate of return for bonds, they are far from perfect investments. First, because you have to pay taxes on Treasury bonds, every time your principal increases to reflect the impact of inflation, the IRS treats the extra value as ordinary income, which is then taxed. Since TIPS protect against inflation by pegging their par values to the Consumer Price Index (CPI) every six months, you could end up paying taxes on phantom income. If the CPI rises 10 percent over the course of six months, for example, a new TIPS bond price would be expected to go from $1,000 to $1,100. That process continues until maturity, so the final value of a TIPS bond can't actually be known until that time. It's also possible that TIPS prices can fall if the CPI falls, but they can never go below the original $1,000 mark. Nevertheless, you're paying taxes along the way.

TIPS are also subject to the same interest rate risk as conventional bonds—if interest rates spike up, the value of your bond will decline and you could face a loss if you don't hold the bond to its maturity. Finally, TIPS are also an implicit bet that investors have correct expectations for inflation—a conventional Treasury bond, for example, that matures in February of 2015 currently yields 4.13 percent, whereas the TIPS bond that also matures in 2015 yields 1.57 percent. This implies that investors believe inflation will run at 2.56 percent per year through 2015. But what if it doesn't? If inflation increases one percent per year through 2015, investors in the regular Treasury bond will have done much better than those in the inflation-protected version. Conversely, if inflation comes in much higher than 2.56 percent per year, the investor in TIPS will do vastly better than an investor in a conventional bond.

Creating a Laddered Bond Portfolio

We are currently emerging from one of the longest periods of declining interest rates in U.S. history. In keeping with the perfect storm analogy, investors are unaccustomed to increasing interest rates, but that is precisely what we might be facing over the next twenty years. As the baby boom generation ages and requires additional medical attention government obligations are going to balloon, adding a huge burden to the Medicare and Medicaid programs. After a long increase in U.S. productivity, many analysts now have more modest expectations for continuing productivity gains, which will directly affect the amount of tax revenue the government collects. Altogether, demographics and tax revenue shortfalls point to an environment in which the government will be forced to increase taxes; the rate of return that investors will demand will in all likelihood increase commensurately.

With this being the case, what should fixed income investors do? We've already seen that intermediate-term bonds outperform long-term bonds in the majority of twenty-year periods analyzed. In an environment of rising interest rates, the best choices are short- and intermediate-term bonds. And the best way to buy them is in a "laddered" fashion.

A laddered portfolio is built by staggering the durations of the bonds you are buying. If you wanted to keep all durations to a maximum of five years, for example, you would buy one bond that matured in one year, the next in two years, and so on, out to the five-year maximum. As each bond matures, you replace it with one that is farthest out on your duration schedule. The staggered maturities allow you to always have funds available for reinvestment. If rates do rise, you will always be putting money to work in the new, higher-interest bonds. My advice would be to do this until interest rates are at or above their historical average. For the period between 1927 and 2004, the average yield on long-term Treasuries is 5.39 percent and 4.88 percent for intermediate-term Treasuries. Only after rates have gone above these averages should you consider buying longer-term bonds with a duration of ten or more years. Even then, you will still benefit from using a laddered approach.

Chapter Five Highlights

◆ Bond prices are easy to predict—as rates fall, bond prices increase; as rates rise, bond prices fall. There are a great variety of bonds, but only U.S. Treasury bonds and bills have no default risk.

◆ Bonds are traditionally viewed as "safe" investments, but the historical data contradicts this. Long-term Treasury bonds have provided negative twenty-year real returns 58 percent of the time for all rolling periods between 1947 and 2004. Over all twenty-year periods analyzed, the average real rate of return for long-term bonds was 0.97 percent per year.

◆ Intermediate-term bonds have historically done better than long-term bonds in all rolling twenty-year periods analyzed. They provided negative real returns in 33 percent of all rolling twenty-year periods, compared to 58 percent of all twenty-year periods for long-term bonds. They also had a higher average real rate of return of 1.32 percent per year. In addition, they had a lower correlation with the S&P 500 and provided more positive returns when stock returns were negative.

◆ U.S. Treasury bills provided an anemic real return of 0.13 percent over all rolling twenty-year periods. They provide negative returns over a third of all the twenty-year periods analyzed and should be expected to only keep pace with inflation.

◆ The real rate of return to long-term bonds reached a historic high of 9.38 percent per year for the twenty years ending in September 2001. This was the result of the high nominal yields in 1981—the highest in a century—and will most likely not happen again in our lifetimes.

◆ The Treasury now offers inflation-protected bonds known as TIPS. They assure that investors will always earn a real return from their investments; their current yield serves as an excellent guide to what the expected rate of return will be for bonds in the future. Currently, the ten-year TIPS bond has a yield of 1.57 percent and the twenty-year a yield of 1.70 percent. These become my bond forecasts through 2025.

◆ The best way to invest in bonds during a rising interest rate environment is to create a short-duration laddered portfolio. This allows you to always have money becoming available to invest in a higher yielding bond.

6

Behavioral Economics:

Why We Know What Isn't So

The same thing happened today that happened
yesterday, only to different people.

—Walter Winchell

"We have met the enemy and he is us," claimed Pogo,
Walt Kelly's famous cartoon character. He could have been talking about investors. I have long contended that in the battle for
investment success, investors are their own worst enemy. I published my first investment research in 1989 in a paper entitled
"Quantitative Models as an Aid in Offsetting Systematic Errors in
Decision-Making." In it, I set out to demonstrate that human beings ultimately determine how stocks are priced. Since we don't
check human nature at the door when entering a stock exchange,
I argued that we could learn a great deal from psychological stud-

ies that proved that in uncertain situations, our judgment is systematically flawed.

The solution I offered was that investors could make much better decisions by using dispassionate quantitative models, whose efficacy had been proven over long periods of time. My belief then—as now—was that we can only make better financial decisions by circumnavigating our human nature. All too frequently, investors ignore logic and reason. When trying to make good investment decisions, investors fall back on their own worst impulses. Fear, ignorance, greed, and hope conspire to rob us of our ability to make sensible, intelligent decisions about the market. We let our feelings overcome reason and take shortcuts that violate all logic. We live in the here and now—not the past or future. This is our greatest roadblock when trying to make good investment choices. Because *today's* information or *today's* catchy headlines get filtered through our emotions, we give them the greatest import, giving far too little import to longer spans of time. What the market did today or this week is quite meaningless to long-term investment performance. In his book *Behavioral Finance: Insights into Irrational Minds and Markets,* James Montier writes:

> This is the world of behavioral finance, a world in which human emotions rule, logic has its place, but markets are moved as much by psychological factors as by information from corporate balance sheets. . . .[T]he models of classical finance are fatally flawed. They fail to produce predictions that are even vaguely close to the outcomes we observe in real financial markets. . . . Of course, now we need some understanding of what causes markets to deviate from their fundamental value. The answer quite simply is human behavior.

Behavioral Finance and Prospect Theory

Behavioral finance is a discipline that has emerged in the last two decades; researchers in this field attempt to explain how emotions and cognitive errors influence investors in the decision-making process. In this chapter, I'll review their major findings and how they relate to the twenty-year financial cycles we see occurring again and again.

Amos Tversky, a Stanford psychology professor (who died in 1996), along with his colleague Daniel Kahneman, a professor at Princeton University, are generally cited as the fathers of behavioral finance. Tversky and Kahneman pioneered psychological and economic studies that revolutionized the scientific approach to decision making. They ultimately won many prestigious awards and honors, including the Nobel Memorial Prize in Economic Sciences, awarded to Kahneman in 2002.

They called their work *prospect theory* and argued that when making decisions under uncertainty, people are not cool, rational, and calculating. In a paper published in 1979, they argued that investors placed different weights on financial gains and losses, being much more distressed by prospective losses than pleased by equivalent gains. In one experiment, Tversky and Kahneman offered their subjects two scenarios. In scenario one subjects could choose option A, a 100 percent chance of winning $50, or option B, a 50 percent chance of winning $100 and a 50 percent chance of winning nothing. In scenario two, option A was a 100 percent chance of losing $50, and option B was a 50 percent chance of losing $100 and a 50 percent chance of losing nothing.

Even though the odds were exactly the same in each scenario, Tversky and Kahneman found that an overwhelming majority of their subjects chose option A in scenario one but option B in scenario two. In other words, people are *risk-averse* when facing gains but *risk-seeking* when facing potential losses. When Tversky and Kahneman manipulated the odds in each scenario, they found that generally, people consider losses twice as painful as gains, and will take on *huge* risks to avoid them. Conversely, they will take very little risk when seeking gains. These findings directly contradict a basic rule of traditional economic theory called *expected utility theory*, which posits that people will always behave rationally and pick the optimum solution when facing a gain or loss.

Tversky and Kahneman replicated these results with a new set of participants who made the same mistakes—leading them to conclude that these errors can be predicted and categorized. Worse news is that even armed with this knowledge, investors keep making the same mistakes over and over again. We are all programmed to believe that while these errors might affect *other people*, we are personally immune. As Kahneman says, "these are cognitive illusions that will not go away just because we know them."

Prospect theory directly explains why people sell their winners too soon and hold their losers too long. Historical financial research shows that, in general, winners continue to win and losers continue to lose (for an in-depth discussion of this, see chapter 15 in my earlier book *What Works on Wall Street*). Yet, because of the way our brains are programmed, when it comes to investment decisions we continually do the opposite of what we should. Prospect theory also explains why investors undervalue investments they perceive as risky and overvalue investments they perceive as certain. Thus, despite the long-term evidence that shows inflation-adjusted T-bills earn almost nothing over long periods of time, investors are far more likely to look at T-bills as the safest investment that they can make.

Fear of Regret

Professors Meir Statman of Santa Clara University and Terry Odean of the University of California at Berkeley have also shown that people are so regretful when a stock they own is losing money that they are reluctant to sell it. In his 1998 paper "Are Investors Reluctant to Realize Their Losses?," published in the *Journal of Finance*, Odean analyzed the trading records for ten thousand accounts at a large discount brokerage house. He found a strong tendency among investors to hold losing investments too long and sell winning investments too soon. Odean writes: "These investors demonstrate a strong preference for realizing winners rather than losers. Their behavior does not appear to be motivated by a desire to rebalance portfolios, or to avoid the higher trading costs of low price stocks. Nor is it justified by subsequent portfolio performance."

Others have hypothesized that the well-established fear of regret is the reason that investors follow the crowd. By doing what everyone else is doing, individual investors can avoid the regret they might feel if they resisted conventional wisdom and wound up being wrong. The market bubble of the late 1990s is a classic example of this: investors were essentially buying stocks of profitless companies, primarily because everyone else was doing it. When it went drastically wrong, well, at least they had a lot of company. As the famous economist John M. Keynes aptly quipped, "people would rather fail conventionally than succeed unconventionally."

Another basic human instinct is the desire to appear intelligent—no one wants to advocate ideas or investments that are at odds with the collective wisdom of Wall Street. As a result, investors consistently get swept up in prevailing trends, for better or—more often—worse. If you think you are immune, look at your own portfolio. Chances are, in both the past and the present it mirrors the market's most popular trends.

What's more, popular trends become self-perpetuating. Optimistic investors are often more than willing to throw money at the fastest-growing segments of the market. This often leads to outright speculation, where capital is too readily provided to unworthy companies. Inevitably, many of these speculative investments fail, setting up a market correction. If prolonged, this downturn leaves investors overly pessimistic and risk-averse. And on it goes.

The Availability Error

Another error investors consistently fall victim to is the availability error. Simply put, people overweight information that is easy to recall. Ease of recall is directly linked to how vivid the information is and how frequently we come into contact with it. Dramatic, colorful, and concrete information is easier to remember and influences the choices we make. Statistics are abstract, boring, and dull. Stories are fun, colorful, and interesting. Which will be easier to remember?

At the top of the bubble, investors were bombarded with colorful, interesting stories of the vast wealth being created in Silicon Valley and other new-economy outposts. CNBC churned out colorful charts of stocks rocketing upward and magazines sang the praises of new-era businessmen. Not to be outdone, *Time* named Amazon.com's founder and CEO Jeff Bezos its 2001 "Person of the Year." In its tribute to Bezos, the magazine said, "It's a revolution. It kills old economics, it kills old companies, it kills old rules." And *Time* wasn't alone—the glories of the new economy and new-era investments were trumpeted everywhere in the media, making these the most available "facts" for investors. And because people overweight the most available information, the majority of investors based their investment decisions on what turned out to be illusions.

We're not just susceptible during boom times, either. In the early 1980s investors shunned stocks because of how poorly they had performed over the previous two decades. All the information available to investors at the time indicated that stocks and bonds were the worst investments you could make. In the early 1980s, Howard Ruff's *How to Prosper During the Coming Bad Years* sat at the top of the national best-seller lists for two years, selling almost 3 million copies and becoming one of the top-selling financial books of all time. His forecast for the 1980s? Gold was headed to over $2,000 an ounce and interest rates were going to exceed 40 percent.

The Halo Effect

Well, you might argue, "I always try to make good investment decisions. I listen to the recommendations of Wall Street's highly regarded analysts—after all, they make big bucks for a reason." But do they? Research by money manager David Dreman has shown that for the most part, analysts' predictions are so far off the mark they are virtually useless. Unfortunately, paying attention to high-profile analysts is also part of our human hard-wiring; it is driven by the *halo effect*.

In his book *Irrationality: Why We Don't Think Straight!* Stuart Sutherland says, "Also related to the availability error is the halo effect. If a person has one salient (available) good trait, his other characteristics are likely to be judged by others as better than they really are." In other words, we tend to judge others on the prestige of their position or distinction of their employer. When an analyst from a blue-chip investment house offers advice, we are inclined to believe that his or her opinions are much better than our own.

Rather than actually questioning the validity of what he is saying, we endow him with abilities he might not possess. Sutherland cites a fascinating study that proved how pernicious the halo effect can be. In the study, two psychologists proved that the halo effect strongly influenced what the editors at several important journals of psychology were willing to publish. According to Sutherland the two psychologists

> *selected from each of 12 well-known journals of psychology one published article that had been written by members of one of the 10 most prestigious psychology departments in the US, such as Harvard or Princeton: in consequence, the authors were mostly eminent psychologists. Next, they changed the authors' names to fictitious ones and their affiliations to those of some imaginary university, such as the Tri-Valley Center for Human Potential. They then went through the articles carefully, and whenever they found a passage that might provide a clue to the real authors, they altered it slightly, while leaving the basic contents unchanged. Each article was then typed and submitted under the imaginary names and affiliations to the very same journal that had originally published it.*
>
> *Of the 12 journals, only three spotted that they had already published the article. This was a grave lapse of memory on the part of the editors and their referees, but then memory is fallible; however, worse was to come. Eight out of the remaining nine articles, all of which had been previously published, were rejected. Moreover, of the 16 referees and eight editors who looked at these eight papers, every single one stated that the paper they examined did not merit publication. This is surely a startling instance of the availability error. It suggests that in deciding whether an article should be published, referees and editors pay more attention to the authors' names and to the standing of the institu-*

*tion to which they belong than they do to the scientific work
reported.*

If the halo effect is this profound in a rigorous setting with academic referees and multiple editors, imagine how it can influence the average investor listening to the advice of a blue-chip stock analyst.

Myopic Loss Aversion and Narrow Framing

Richard Thaler is a professor of economics at the University of Chicago and one of the more prolific authors in the study of behavioral finance. In his paper "Myopic Loss Aversion and the Equity Premium Puzzle," he and coauthor Shlomo Benartzi argue that investors do not invest their money rationally or with the appropriate time horizons in mind. For example, if a young investor is saving for retirement thirty years from now, he should use that time period as his benchmark for investment returns.

Unfortunately, investors rarely do this. Instead, Thaler and Benartzi found that if investors are in the habit of checking their portfolio every quarter, *that* becomes their new time horizon. They make choices based on their portfolio's recent performance rather than focusing on the twenty or thirty years they have until retirement. Thus, our young investor will not be able to make wise choices if he remains myopically focused on the short term. The combination of shortsighted behavior and an aversion to loss helps explain why many people find higher-returning, higher-risk stock funds less attractive than they should.

When looking at investment alternatives, how you frame a problem can strongly affect the outcome. I tested this by showing people two graphs, featured in figures 6–1 and 6–2, asking which portfolio was more attractive to them. When presented with the annual returns featured in figure 6–1, most people chose the less volatile portfolio with steady year-in, year-out gains. However, when presented with figure 6–2, showing the cumulative value of $10,000 invested in exactly the same portfolio, most chose the more volatile portfolio that offered higher returns over the long term.

This exercise shows how strongly framing affects us as investors. When we look at the day-to-day or even year-to-year changes in our portfolios, the narrower time frame makes us very risk averse. When we use a broader time frame that only takes final value into account, however, we are far more likely to invest in the portfolio that appears risky in the short term but provides much higher returns over the long term.

Framing and shortsightedness are also the reasons investors prefer stocks that have done very well over the last five years—when they should be doing just the opposite. In a study I conducted for *What Works on Wall Street*, I looked at the returns of the stocks that had either been the fifty best performers over the last five years or the fifty worst performers. The results showed that an investment in the fifty *worst* performing stocks from the previous five years trounced an investment in the fifty best performing stocks. One dollar invested in the previous five years' worst performing stocks on December 31, 1955, grew to $248.12 by the end of 2003, a real annual return of 12.17 percent. The same dollar invested in the previous five years' best performing stocks grew to only $3.56, a real annual return of just 2.68 percent per year!

These data have also proved true in international markets. In the essay "The Psychology of Underreaction and Overreaction in World Equity Markets," published in *Security Market Imperfections in World Wide Equity Markets*, Professor Werner F. M. De Bondt finds the same pattern in ten countries, from Australia to the United Kingdom. De Bondt says: "How valid are expert and amateur predictions of share prices, earnings, etc.? How do people go

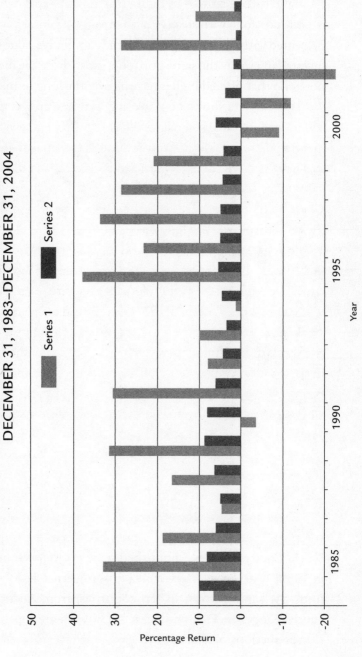

FIGURE 6-1 NOMINAL ANNUAL RETURNS, TWO DIFFERENT PORTFOLIOS, DECEMBER 31, 1983–DECEMBER 31, 2004

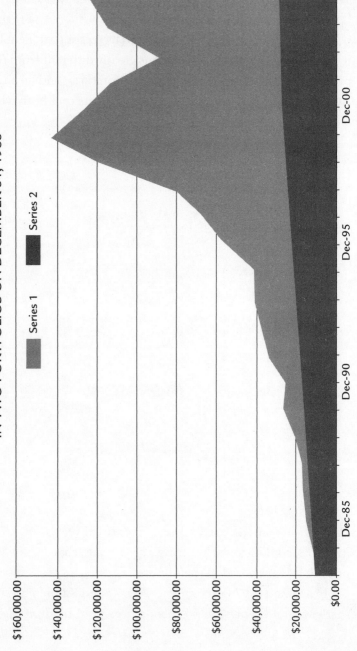

FIGURE 6-2 TERMINAL NOMINAL VALUE OF $10,000 INVESTMENT IN TWO PORTFOLIOS ON DECEMBER 31, 1983

about making these forecasts? What type of information attracts the most attention? A recurring theme in the literature is the disposition to predict the future based on the recent past. People find it difficult to project anything that is greatly different from the apparent trend—even if over-optimistic forecasts and groundless confidence are the net result." He also suggests that both winning and losing stocks may simply be reverting to their mean returns.

Clearly, the best way to make an investment decision is to study *all* periods that coincide with your actual investment horizon. If you are forty-five and want to retire at sixty-five, then you should look at all twenty-year periods to make your choices, but human nature makes this highly unlikely. We attach the most importance to the news we read today, and by doing so lose sight of the bigger picture.

Mental Anchoring

Behavioral finance also shows that we use recent prices and news as mental anchors for what price levels or returns are "right." For example, people have a strong tendency to overweight recent experience, view it as "correct" and then extrapolate it well into the future. This helps explain why investors in the late 1990s believed that large-cap growth and technology stocks were the only game in town. Mental anchoring also traps us into believing that whatever is happening in the market today will continue forever, rather than doing what it always does and returning to its long-term mean. The NASDAQ may not reach 5,000 for years, but for many investors coming of age during the bubble, that is the "right" price that is anchored in their brains.

In a famous 1974 experiment, Tversky and Kahneman showed that you could get people to anchor answers to random numbers. They asked a group of participants to guess how many African countries were members of the United Nations. Before being allowed to guess, however, the psychologists spun a fortune wheel with numbers between 1 and 100. Unbeknownst to the participants, the wheel was rigged to land on either 10 or 65. After the spin, the participants were asked if the actual number of African nations was higher or lower than the number on the wheel, and for their exact guess. The median response from the group that guessed after the wheel landed on 10 was 25; the median guess from the group that guessed after the wheel landed on 65 was 45!

Overconfidence and Hindsight Bias

Each of us, it seems, believes that we are above average. Sadly, this cannot be statistically true. Yet in tests of people's belief in their own ability (typically people are asked to rank their ability as a driver), virtually *everyone* puts themselves in the upper 10 to 20 percent! Other surveys show that when you take a random sample of adult males, and ask them to rate themselves on a number of parameters, the first being their ability to get along with others, *every single respondent* ranked himself in the top 10 percent of the population; and a full 25 percent say they fall in the top 1 percent! Similarly, 70 percent ranked themselves at the top for leadership ability, and only 2 percent felt they were below average leaders. Finally—in an area where self-deception should be difficult—60 percent of males said that they were in the top 20 percent for athletic ability, and only 6 percent said they were below average. We are clearly deluding ourselves.

In his 1997 paper "The Psychology of the Non-Professional Investor," Nobel laureate Daniel Kahneman says: "The biases of judgment and decision making have sometimes been called cognitive illusions. Like visual illusions, the mistakes of intuitive reasoning are not easily eliminated. . . . Merely learning about illusions does not eliminate them." Kahneman goes on to say that, like our investors above, the majority of investors are dramatically over-confident and optimistic, prone to an illusion of control where none exists. Kahneman also points out that the reason it is so difficult for investors to correct these false beliefs is because they also suffer from *hindsight bias*. Kahneman writes that "psychological evidence indicates people can rarely reconstruct, after the fact, what they thought about the probability of an event before it occurred. Most are honestly deceived when they exaggerate their earlier estimate of the probability that the event would occur. . . . Because of another hindsight bias, events that the best-informed experts did not anticipate often appear almost inevitable after they occur."

In a famous experiment, a Cornell professor gave his class a quiz at the beginning of the year, asking them to forecast where financial indicators like the Dow Jones Industrial Average, interest rates, and gold prices would be at the end of the year. He put the forecasts away until the end of the term, when he then asked if anyone recalled their forecasts. Most only vaguely recalled the assignment. In this particular year, the Dow had been strong, with falling interest rates and stable inflation. When the professor asked how many thought they had made correct forecasts, virtually *every* hand in the room went up. However, when the actual forecasts were reviewed, they were all over the map, with many predicting a *falling* Dow and *rising* interest rates! Just like the Cornell students, investors frequently deceive themselves into thinking they *knew* something would happen before it did. In reality, this is rarely true.

Representativeness

We often assume things will come out the way we think they should—stocks with great performance should have great stories driving their gains. Great companies should be great investments;

boring companies should be boring investments. In forming subjective judgments people look for familiar patterns, relying on well-worn stereotypes. These mental shortcuts are called *heuristics,* or mental rules of thumb. In many instances, these mental shortcuts are helpful, but not when it comes to investing. Here, they frequently lead to errors in judgment. We've seen, for example, that people largely ignore how frequently something occurs. These odds are called *base rates.* Base rates are among the most illuminating statistics that exist. They're just like batting averages. For example, if a town of 100,000 people had 70,000 lawyers and 30,000 librarians, the base rate for lawyers in that town is 70 percent. When used in the stock market, base rates tell you what to expect from a certain *class* of stocks (e.g., all stocks with high dividend yields) and what that variable *generally* predicts for the future. But base rates tell you *nothing* about how each *individual* member of that class will behave.

Most statistical prediction techniques use base rates. Seventy-five percent of university students with grade point averages above 3.5 go on to do well in graduate school. Smokers are twice as likely to get cancer. Stocks with low price-to-earnings ratios outperform the market 65 percent of the time. The best way to predict the future is to bet with the base rate that is derived from a large sample. Yet numerous studies have found that people make full use of base rate information *only* when there is a lack of descriptive data. In one example, people are told that out of a sample of 100 people, 70 are lawyers and 30 are engineers. When provided with no additional information and asked to guess the occupation of a randomly selected 10, people use the base rate information, saying all 10 are lawyers, since by doing so they assure themselves of getting the most right.

However, when worthless but descriptive data is added, such as "Dick is a highly motivated thirty-year-old married man who is well liked by his colleagues," people largely ignore the base rate information in favor of their "feel" for the person. They are certain that their unique insights will help them make a better forecast, even when the additional information is meaningless. We prefer descriptive data to impersonal statistics because it better represents our individual experience. When stereotypical information is added, such as "Dick is thirty years old, married, shows no interest in politics or social issues and likes to spend free time on his many hobbies which include carpentry and mathematical puzzles," people *totally* ignore the base rate and bet Dick is an engineer, despite the 70 percent chance that he is a lawyer. One can even jack the base rate for lawyers up to over 90 percent, and people will cling to their stereotypical opinion of an engineer.

Behavioral Finance and the Twenty-Year Money Cycle

Such is the state of *Homo economicus*—even though we can learn and rationally understand why we make the investing mistakes we do, we are destined to repeat them. We are hard-wired to act the way we do. Neurobiologists are proving this with PET scans of our brains—when making decisions under uncertainty the rational part of the brain is mostly dormant but the emotional part fires away! In his book *Mean Markets and Lizard Brains*, Terry Burnham says that there are biological causes for irrational financial behavior, and these in turn cause market panics and crashes. We literally are reverting to our "lizard brain" when faced with the emotion-jarring task of investing our money. He points out what a recent study at MIT confirmed—the most successful investors are those who have a system in place to guard against emotional decisions.

Indeed, having a guiding, unemotional system might be the *only* way to successfully guard against making the same mistakes time and again. As Woody Dorsey says in his book *Behavioral Trading: Methods for Measuring Investor Confidence, Expectations, and Market Trends:* "What is the difference between hunter-gatherer guys and gals of 40,000 years ago and our contemporary go-getters? Nothing. The competitive urge is basic and perpetual."

Financial markets have alternated between booms and busts for over two hundred years. Each generation falls prey to the fads, fallacies, enthusiasms, and stories of its era, most often when the market is at or near the end of one cycle and the beginning of the next. The problem is, investors make decisions based on information they learned about as it unfolded—information that proves nearly useless in the market's next phase. This explains why investors so predictably shun stocks and bonds near market bottoms but buy with abandon near market tops. It seems each generation is amused by the folly of those that preceded it, while remaining totally ignorant of its own.

To understand that our earlier theories of rational human decision-making were fatally flawed, we must pay attention to the actual data and the actual way we make choices. As Maurice Allais, the eminent French economist and winner of the 1988 Nobel Prize for Economics, says, "I have never hesitated to question commonly accepted theories when they appeared to me to be founded on hypotheses which implied consequences incompatible with observed data. Dominant ideas, however erroneous they may be, end up, simply through repetition, by acquiring the quality of established truths which cannot be questioned without confronting the active ostracism of the establishment."

By ignoring all of the experimental data that has accumulated over the last fifty years, we continually put ourselves in harm's way, and continue to make exactly the same mistakes, generation after generation. It seems our very humanity is what makes this endless cycle a permanent facet of our investment lives.

Chapter Six Highlights

◆ Modern portfolio theory contends that investors are rational, dispassionate, and understand the odds. Fifty years of financial evidence and behavioral research contradicts this theory.

◆ Behavioral finance is a new discipline that attempts to define the way investors *actually* make choices. Researchers have found that in reality, people regularly violate the basic rules of rational decision-making.

◆ Behavioral finance research shows that investors are risk-averse when facing gains but risk-seeking when facing losses. Investors also overweight recent information—especially when it is colorful and vivid—and have a strong tendency to follow current market trends.

◆ Investors face a number of psychological pitfalls. Most of us are guilty of:

1. Shortsightedness—our overreliance on short-term data

2. Overconfidence—the tendency to rank our own abilities too highly

3. Hindsight bias—believing that we know an outcome before it occurs

4. Representativeness—seeing things the way we think they "ought" to be.

◆ Investors' behavior can often be best described as bipolar. On one hand, they are overly timid, risk-averse, and prone to follow the crowd. On the other hand, they are far too confident and optimistic. The modulation between the two may explain the market's boom-bust cycle.

◆ Given the predictability of investors' behavior—both historically and internationally—it appears to be a fundamental part of human nature. In order to overcome the enemy within, planning and structure are essential to investment success.

7

Demographic Trends: Friend or Foe?

For every thing there is a season, and a time for
every purpose under the heaven.

.—Ecclesiastes

Over the last decade there has been a burgeoning interest in the effects that demographic patterns have on the economy
and stock market, with many popular books and academic papers
finding important connections between the two. In their book *The
Fourth Turning: What the Cycles of History Tell Us About America's Next
Rendezvous with Destiny,* William Strauss and Neil Howe write that
the human life cycle is a predictable chronology of 1) Childhood;
2) Young adulthood; 3) Midlife; and 4) Elderhood. Each of these
phases coincides with predictable patterns of earning, spending,
saving, and investing. According to Strauss, Howe, and other
acolytes of demographic destiny, understanding where our economy is headed is a simple matter of analyzing demographics, since

where each group is in their life cycle will determine what they will be doing and how they will be investing and spending in the future.

According to Harry Dent Jr., in his book *The Next Great Bubble Boom: How to Profit from the Greatest Boom in History; 2005–2009*, "The point is that there is a new information-based science built on predictable cause-and-effect impacts of how we change as we age that is just as predictable on average as life insurance actuarial tables for when we will die. . . . Demographics as a new science is the greatest breakthrough we have seen in economics."

Dent and others cite simple facts to support their arguments. For example, consumer spending accounts for approximately 60 to 70 percent of gross domestic product, with the biggest spenders between the ages forty-five and fifty-four. You can therefore make very accurate predictions regarding the economy and the stock market by looking at how many people there are at any given time between ages forty-five and fifty-four, and how many there will be at various points in the future.

Demographic Demons

After establishing that the majority of gross domestic product is the result of consumer spending in his book *The Great Bust Ahead*, Daniel Arnold succinctly concludes:

> Now that we know that we are responsible for the GDP, it is only common sense that "who we are" must have a powerful bearing on the GDP. For example, if we were all fifteen years old with virtually nothing to spend, the GDP would be pathetic. If on the other hand we were all forty years old with good incomes (and spending it all as we do) the economy would be going gangbusters. So, at any given time, the more of us with

more money to spend there are, the better the economy (GDP) is going to be. *[Emphasis in original]*

Both Arnold and Dent then plot out how many big spenders there are in the country at any given time. To their eyes this presents a perfect picture of how well the economy—and by extension the stock market—will be performing in the years ahead.

Using these simple facts, the most popular books on demographics come to similar conclusions: the 78 million baby boomers—the largest generation in U.S. history—will drive the stock market to new heights through 2009 or 2010 but then bring it crashing down as they enter retirement and sell their stocks. According to the demographic data, the trend does not turn positive again until the year 2021 when the echo-boom generation starts hitting their peak spending years.

It Works—Until It Doesn't

The problem with the approach advocated by Dent and Arnold is that the inflation-adjusted Dow Jones Industrial Average *does* broadly mirror the number of forty-five-to-fifty-four-year-olds in the population *until* about 1987, when the correlation between demographics and the Dow becomes much fuzzier. Both Dent and Arnold start "adjusting" the data to make the two correlate more highly again—first it's technology innovation, then it's the introduction of the birth control pill which allowed baby boomers to delay parenthood and therefore their peak spending years, then it's that in the 1990s the preferred index was not the Dow but the NASDAQ, and on and on.

Whatever the reason, demographic patterns began diverging from the DJIA in 1987—and they haven't gotten back in sync since.

The impulse to tweak and adjust the data is understandable, but doesn't always make sense. For example, both authors point out that the NASDAQ got the lion's share of investors' money at the height of the tech boom in the late 1990s, arguing that is the reason the Dow didn't do as well. Yet they conveniently ignore that the same was true for the AMEX stock exchange in the late 1960s: during *that* bubble the AMEX went up at six times the rate of the Dow.

Remember hindsight bias from the last chapter? If you continually adjust the graphs as "new" data becomes available, the charts will show perfect correlation *after* the fact but will be of little use to users *now*. For example, say foreign investors start aggressively buying U.S. securities in the next several years. While that is something that is very difficult to predict now, it might seem obvious after the fact, tempting the Dent school of demographers to once again use *hindsight* to adjust their charts to reflect these new buyers. Unfortunately, the new trend will have provided zero *predictive* information in real time. Without these ongoing modifications, the data doesn't seem to hold up. According to the chart on page 21 in Dent's *The Next Great Bubble Boom,* if the Dow truly mirrored the immigration-adjusted births as of 2005, it would currently be trading at nearly 20,000, not the actual 10,500 level it was at in the summer of 2005.

Talking 'Bout My Generation

Part of the problem may be the baby boomers themselves. Who's to say that they will actually behave like the generations that preceded them when deciding how to invest or behave during retirement? In each of their previous cycles, boomers have acted very differently from those who came before them, from their hippie, antiestablishment youths to their embrace of individualism and entrepreneurship in middle age. Thus far, they have defied prediction. According to a new report called *New Retirement Survey* conducted by Ken Dychtwald for Merrill Lynch, boomers will likely continue their rebellious ways right through retirement. Dychtwald finds that the long-held assumptions about retirement—that it begins at sixty-two, that it's spent pursuing leisure activities, and that people accumulate most of their savings for it before age fifty—are all *wrong* in regard to the baby boomers. It turns out that baby boomers born in 1946 (who are now approaching the age of sixty) did the bulk of their retirement saving and investing *after* turning fifty, and the majority of them expect to continue working well past the normal retirement age of sixty-five. The baby boomers are turning the accepted notion of what a "typical" retiree looks like on its head. As a result, the era of age-based assumptions may be ending.

Baby boomers may also buck their forebears by continuing to embrace stocks rather than bonds as their preferred investments during retirement. Unlike their parents' generation, they have a deeply embedded belief that stocks are the best long-term investments, and as they consider their expanding longevity, they may fear the relative penury that a bonds-only portfolio might offer. They are also the Peter Pan generation that continues, well into their fifties and sixties, to redefine what it means to be "old"—in their case, five to ten years from whatever age they are now!

It has also been convenient for demographers to look at baby boomers as one monolithic cohort. There are actually large differences among them, depending upon when they were born. Demographer Jonathan Pontell has gone so far as to separate the baby boom into two groups: the traditional boomers whom he assigns the birth years 1946–1956 and the group he calls "Generation Jones," or those born between 1956 and 1964. According to Pontell, the two subgroups have very little in common, possess very different attitudes about life and work, and have very different ideas about how to achieve what they want in life. It doesn't take much imagination to see that these differences might lead to very different investment and retirement strategies.

Academic Debate

The academic debate about the impact of current demographic trends has been fierce, with two camps emerging: the first claims that demographics are destiny; the second that the aging of the baby boomers will have very little effect on the stock market. The stakes in this debate are enormous, since the baby boomers are the largest generation *ever* in American history and therefore will have a potentially huge impact on the stock market in the years to come.

On the side of "demographics as destiny" are many luminaries such as Jeremy Siegel, author of *Stocks for the Long Run,* Robert Shiller, author of *Irrational Exuberance,* and a trio of finance professors who have published a paper called "Demography and the Long-Run Predictability of the Stock Market." The authors—John Geanakoplos of Yale University, Michael Magill of the University of Southern California, and Martine Quinzii of the University of California at Davis—rely less on the absolute number of big spenders than Dent and his ilk, but nevertheless claim that demographics are the most important factor in determining long-term trends for stock prices. The authors note that "since the turn of the century, the live births in the US have also gone through alternating *twenty-year phases of baby booms and baby busts:* for example, the low birth rate during the Great Depression was followed by the Baby Boom of the fifties and the subsequent Baby Bust of the seventies. These birth waves have resulted in systematic temporal changes in the age composition of the population in the postwar period, *roughly corresponding to the twenty-year phases of the stock market.*" [Emphasis added.] In other words, we see the same boom and bust phenomena in the birthrate as we do in the stock market. Perhaps one causes the other.

Unlike Dent, who plots the absolute number of boomers with an expected correlation with absolute returns for equity markets, the academics have identified a ratio that seems fairly predictive of the market's future: the ratio of middle-aged to young investors. While the professors don't claim their model will forecast the exact levels of the Dow Jones Industrial Average or the S&P 500, they argue that when the ratio of middle-aged to young investors *increases,* the market's PE ratio increases, and when the ratio decreases the market's PE ratio decreases. While their ratio only *generally* predicts what price investors will be willing to pay for every dollar of earnings, it did accurately predict the great boom between 1982 and 2000, when both the ratio and PE's were rising. The ratio is now predicting falling PE ratios as the ratio of middle-aged to young investors declines. Their model also works in markets outside of the United States, predicting the massive decline in Japanese stock prices as the ratio in Japan peaked in the late 1980s and went into decline all through the 1990s and early 2000s. The professors say that the ratio will be declining in the United States until 2018, when it will again turn strongly positive, as the huge echo-boom generation enters the investment fray.

Consistent with Reversion to the Mean

These findings are similar to the Leuthold Group's in chapter 2, the difference here being that the professors find demographics to be the driving force in the expansion and contraction of the PE ratio. John Y. Campbell and Robert J. Shiller offer similar findings in their March 2001 paper "Valuation Ratios and the Long-Run Stock Market Outlook: An Update." In it they find that the relative level of PE ratios and dividend yields is useful in predicting future returns, with high PE ratios and low dividend yields leading to below average future performance and low PE ratios and high dividend yields leading to above average returns. This hypothesis is consistent with both reversion to the mean and the demographic argument offered by Geanakoplos, Magill, and Quinzii in their paper.

Demographics Don't Matter

On the other side of the debate are a group of academics who believe that demographic data is useless when forecasting stock market returns. Robin Brooks, an economist at the International Monetary Fund, claims that it's not the behavior of all the baby boomers that matters; it's what the richest among them decide to do. In an extension of the 80/20 rule, where 20 percent of the people are responsible for 80 percent of the results, Brooks argues that only the actions of the largest equity holders will really matter. He believes that even if a majority of baby boomers are forced to sell their stocks and mutual funds during retirement, they will still account for only a modest percentage of the markets' dollar volume, since few have saved enough to be entirely self-sufficient during retirement. Brooks points out that the majority of baby boomers will be reliant on the government for much of their retirement income.

Data from the Federal Reserve back up Dr. Brooks's claim. In 2001, the richest 1 percent of the U.S. population owned 53 percent of the stock owned by individuals and the richest 10 percent owned 88 percent. Brooks claims that corporations will likely raise their dividends in order to keep these rich owners happy, leading to an era in which dividends are, once again, an important force behind stock returns.

Demographics Do Matter

In the end, it is difficult to argue that 78 million Americans moving into retirement will not have an impact on both the economy and the stock market. Perhaps one of the reasons the Dow is currently at 10,500 rather than the 20,000 that Dent's demographics suggest is that the market has *already* begun factoring the demographic shift into prices. This is, after all, one of the most hotly debated stock market issues of our day, and the market usually factors such data into current share prices. But Dr. Brooks's forecast could be equally true—if shareholders start clamoring for stocks with higher dividend yields, companies eager to keep their stock prices up will do everything in their power to deliver these yields.

The most important point is that the 78 million boomers *will* affect the market and which types of stocks are rewarded. Just as surely, over the next twenty years the cost of Medicare and Medicaid will soar, as will shortfalls in the Social Security trust fund after 2018. This will probably lead to higher taxes, reduced payouts, and other Draconian measures. Huge governmental deficits and increasing taxes are rarely stock-friendly environments, so even if boomers hold on to their stocks, the very size of their demographic appears certain to affect the stock and bond markets in numerous ways.

Demographics Affect Our Destiny

Demographics were clearly a strong tailwind to the bull market between 1982 and 2000; they now appear poised to act more like a headwind. Short of dramatic changes in U.S. entitlement programs, the government will face unprecedented challenges as the 78 million boomers move into retirement and old age. This will inevitably lead to tax increases and benefit reductions—hardly an environment conducive to double-digit stock market returns. And even if boomers choose to stick with stocks, they will most likely choose those that pay hefty dividends and offer greater price stability. And while it is unlikely that the doomsayers' prophecies will come true with the age wave crashing into a great new depression, the age wave is nevertheless unavoidable, and very consistent with what mean reversion and contraction of PE ratios forecast for markets over the next twenty years.

Chapter Seven Highlights

- ◆ Demographic trends affect both the economy and stock market. Author Harry Dent believes that the stock market closely follows the number of high-spending forty-nine-year olds present in the economy. According to Dent, once that demographic peaks in 2009, the stock market will decline until the number of high-spending forty-nine-year-olds expands once again.

- ◆ There are two academic schools of thought about demographic influences. The first finds a relationship between the ratio of middle-aged investors to younger investors. They believe that as this ratio is rising, the PE ratio of the market expands and stock prices rise. When this ratio is falling the PE ratio contracts and the market limps along. The ratio between middle-aged and younger investors is now falling, and will not turn upward again until 2018.

  The second school sees no relationship between demographics and the stock market. According to this school, only the actions of the minority of investors with the majority of assets affect the valuation of the stock market.

◆ Even if demographics have no direct effect on the market's valuation, the unprecedented number of baby boomers approaching retirement will affect both the government's ability to pay retirement and health care benefits and the types of stocks that aging baby boomers will demand.

8

Roll Your Own: Using Stock Selection
Strategies to Improve the Odds

*Take the course opposite to custom and you will
almost always do well.*

—Jean-Jacques Rousseau

Having made my case for the wisdom of investing in
small-cap stocks and large-cap value stocks over the next twenty
years, let's now review how you may further enhance a portfolio of
these broad categories of stocks. In my book *What Works on Wall
Street,* I examined fifty-three years of data to see which stock selection strategies consistently outperformed the market. My research
revealed that there were many strategies that provided far higher
returns than simple indexes like the S&P 500 or a small-cap index
like the Russell 2000. In this chapter, I will examine two large-cap

value strategies, a large-cap growth strategy with a value parameter, and two small-cap strategies. This will give you the ability to concentrate your portfolio in the styles that should work best over the next two decades while improving returns by utilizing superior strategies. I will also look at an all-capitalization strategy that has historically provided excellent returns with low levels of risk. Readers interested in a more thorough evaluation of a full spectrum of strategies should consult the third edition of *What Works on Wall Street.*

Just like when we reviewed the rolling twenty-year real rates of returns of the S&P 500 and the Fama/French–style indexes, it is vital to examine as much data as possible for these stock selection strategies. For all but three, we have fifty-three years of annual data and forty-one years of monthly data. Remember that because of the "noise" generated through shorter-term market gyrations, it is only the fullness of time that allows superior strategies to reveal themselves. It's vital to understand that the day-to-day ups and downs of a strategy have little bearing on how it will perform over longer periods of time. I am always looking for strategies that have outperformed their indexes over all rolling three-, five-, ten-, and twenty-year periods. And to show you how certain strategies can serve as excellent proxies for the indexes we examined, let's start with the one for which we have the most data.

The Dogs of the Dow: An Excellent Ten-Stock Proxy for the Fama/French Large Value Index

The first strategy we'll look at is the "Dogs of the Dow," which is made up of stocks from the Dow Jones Industrial Average. Created in 1928 by the editors of the *Wall Street Journal,* the modern DJIA consists of the thirty companies that the editors deem to be the best representatives of large, well-known U.S. corporations. Currently, it includes such household names as American Express, Citigroup, Coca-Cola, GE, GM, Intel, and Microsoft. The average is continually updated to include the largest titans of corporate America. Because of its long history, we have a hefty seventy-six years of data to examine for the Dogs of the Dow strategy. I published my original research on this strategy in *Barron's* in 1992 in an article entitled "High Yields, High Rewards: An Uncomplicated Way to Beat the Market."

The strategy is as simple as they come. Once a year, you rank the thirty stocks in the Dow by their dividend yield and buy the ten stocks with the highest yields. After doing so, you wait one year, re-rank the stocks by dividend yield, and replace those stocks that have fallen off the list with the new highest-yielding stocks. Despite its utter simplicity, this ten-stock strategy has beaten the S&P 500 in all but three rolling ten-year periods between 1929 and 2004, and even then it only slightly underperformed the S&P 500. Better yet, the strategy outperformed the S&P 500 in *all* rolling twenty-year periods. Its returns are extremely similar to those of the Fama/French Large Value Index reviewed in chapter 4.

Over the seventy-six years between December 31, 1928, and December 31, 2004, the Dogs of the Dow strategy provided a real average annual return of 8.63 percent, turning one dollar invested at the end of 1928 into $541.50 by the end of 2004. Over the same period, the Fama/French Large Value Index provided a real average annual return of 8.24 percent, turning one dollar into $410.84, and the S&P 500 had a real average annual return of 6.29 percent, turning one dollar invested into $103.43. As measured by the standard deviation of return, the risk of the Dogs of the Dow strategy was 21.06 percent, similar to the 20.04 percent risk of the S&P 500. Thus, on risk-adjusted basis, the Dogs of the Dow strategy is more attractive than the Fama/French Large Value Index, which had a standard deviation of return of 27.05 percent. Figure 8–1 shows the real growth of one dollar for all three strategies.

Now look at the Dogs of the Dow strategy's twenty-year rolling returns. The lowest return was 2.92 percent; the highest was 14.35 percent and the average for all rolling twenty-year periods was 10.07 percent. Note that with large-cap value strategies like this, you can buy as few as ten stocks and still have an adequately diversified portfolio. (With the smaller capitalization strategies we'll look at later in the chapter, you'll need to own more stocks in order to reduce volatility.) Figure 8–2 shows the rolling twenty-year real rate of return for the Dogs of the Dow and Fama/French Value Index. Note here that because we only have annual data for the DJIA back to 1928, the graph is less inclusive than those using monthly data featured earlier in the book.

Dogs of the Dow Twenty-Year Outlook

The Dogs of the Dow strategy is an extremely effective way to buy out-of-favor blue-chip stocks that also offer high dividend yields. Because its historical returns are very similar to those of the Fama/French Large Value Index, my forecast for the high-yielding Dow stocks is the same as that for large-cap value stocks, specifically a real rate of return between 6.03 and 8.03 percent over the next twenty years. As I write this in the summer of 2005, the stocks include GM, Verizon, Merck, Citigroup, and Coca-Cola and the ten-stock list sports a current dividend yield of 4.1 percent. I'll explain how you can find and buy the high-yielding Dow stocks in chapter 12.

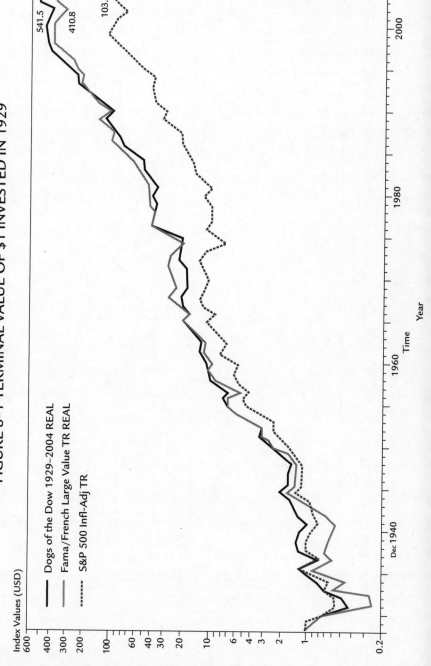

FIGURE 8–1 TERMINAL VALUE OF $1 INVESTED IN 1929

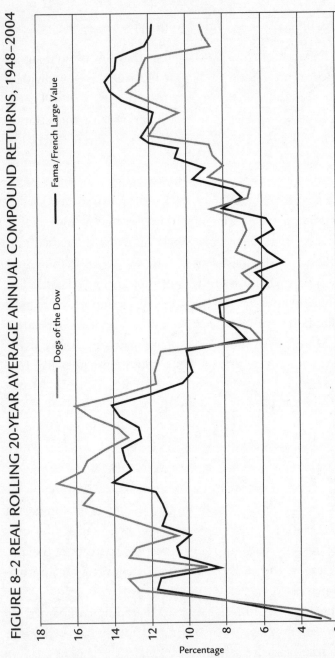

FIGURE 8-2 REAL ROLLING 20-YEAR AVERAGE ANNUAL COMPOUND RETURNS, 1948–2004

Improving on Large-Cap Value Returns

I'll now look at another simple strategy that has offered significantly higher returns than the simple Dogs of the Dow dividend
yield strategy. Because it was created using the S&P COMPUSTAT
database, I only have data going back to 1951 for this strategy.
Featured in *What Works on Wall Street,* this Market Leaders Low
Price–to–Cash Flow strategy buys the ten market-leading companies with the lowest price–to–cash flow ratios. I define market-
leading companies as nonutility stocks with greater than average
market capitalization, shares outstanding, cash flow, and sales 50
percent greater than the average stock. Applying these factors to
the COMPUSTAT database I used for *What Works on Wall Street*
leaves just 6 percent of the stocks from the entire COMPUSTAT
universe qualifying as Market Leaders. It is important to note
that Market Leaders allow the inclusion of American Depository
Receipts (ADRs), which are dollar-denominated overseas shares
that trade in the United States. Thus, giant companies like Ger-
many's Deutsche Telekom, Japan's NTT, and the United Kingdom's British Petroleum are available for consideration. This is an
important distinction, especially when comparing performance
with the S&P 500 and the French and Fama Value Index, which
are made up of only U.S. companies. In the new global economy,
the ability to purchase shares of companies domiciled outside the
United States might be an advantage. Indeed, the number of
ADRs in the Market Leaders universe has grown considerably over
time—in 1995, they made up approximately 20 percent of the universe, whereas at the end of 2004 they accounted for approximately 35 percent.

After creating the universe of market-leading companies, we
sort the universe by price–to–cash flow and buy the ten stocks with
the *lowest* price-to-cash flow ratios to create the Market Leaders

Low Price-to-Cash Flow portfolio. Once a year, we update the strategy, replacing any stocks that have fallen off the list with the new lowest price-to-cash flow large-cap stocks. Over fifty-three years this strategy has significantly outperformed simple large-cap value indexes.

For the fifty-three years between December 31, 1951, and December 31, 2004, the strategy provided a real average annual compound return of 14.33 percent, turning one dollar invested in 1951 into $1,211.06 at the end of 2004. That's significantly higher than the return of the Fama/French Large Value Index, which earned a real average annual compound return of 9.69 percent over the same period. One dollar invested in the Fama/French Large Value Index grew to $134.74 over the same period. For comparative purposes, the S&P 500 earned a real average annual compound return of 7.43 percent over the period, turning one dollar invested in 1951 into $44.68 at the end of 2004. Figure 8–3 shows the returns for each of the strategies. Risk, as measured by the standard deviation of return, was higher for this strategy than the Fama/French Large Value Index: this strategy's standard deviation was 25.55 versus 21.93 for the Fama/French series.

Twenty-Year Rolling Results Better than Fama/French Index and Forecast

When we extend the holding period to twenty years, we see that Market Leaders Low Price-to-Cash Flow has consistently done much better than both the S&P 500 and the Fama/French Large Value Index. Remembering that we have more limited data and must start the rolling twenty-year real compound returns analysis in 1971, we see that the minimum return was 6.64 percent per year; the maximum return was 17.91 percent per year and the average real average annual compound return was 12.47 percent.

FIGURE 8-3 TERMINAL VALUE OF $1 INVESTED IN 1952

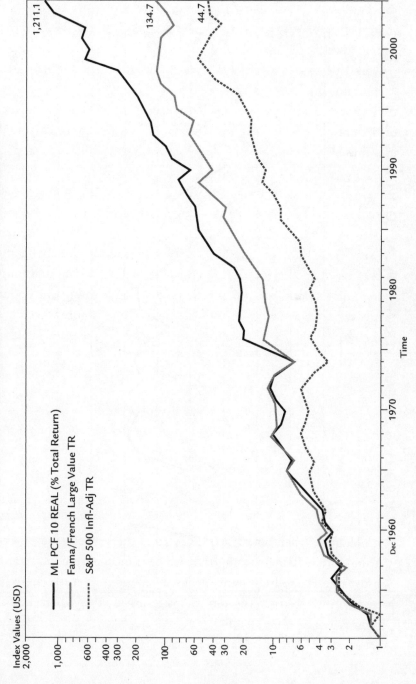

Index Values (USD)

ML PCF 10 REAL (% Total Return)
Fama/French Large Value TR
S&P 500 Infl-Adj TR

Time

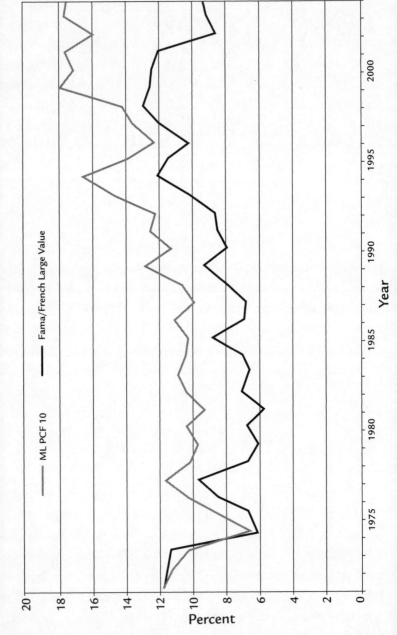

FIGURE 8-4 REAL ROLLING 20-YEAR AVERAGE ANNUAL COMPOUND RETURNS, 1971–2004

Figure 8–4 shows the rolling twenty-year real compound returns for the strategy and the Fama/French index. On average, this strategy did 3.33 percent better than the Fama/French index for all rolling twenty-year periods. Adding this premium to our forecast for the Fama/French Large Value Index (between 6.03 and 8.03 percent annually over the next twenty years), I arrive at an expected rate of return for stocks meeting the Market Leaders Low Price–to–Cash Flow requirements of between 9.36 and 11.36 percent through 2022–2025.

Caveats for Concentrated Strategies

Things look much improved when you use style-specific strategies, but each strategy comes with several caveats. First, even though these are all large-cap stock strategies, when you own only ten stocks you should expect greater volatility than you would experience with a more broadly diversified index. For example, year-to-year volatility can be high, as 1990 demonstrated—in a year when value stocks did poorly, this strategy lost 26.69 percent while the S&P 500 dropped a more modest 8.74 percent. If you have a true twenty-year time horizon, you should be prepared for dispersion like this. Happily, however, this dispersion is found more often at the other extreme, as in 2003 when this strategy's stocks soared 87.7 percent compared to a more modest rise of 26.32 percent for the S&P 500.

The second caveat is that these types of strategies tend to choose companies that appear rather ugly to investors at first blush. For example, the current list is concentrated in the rather dowdy and unappealing automobile and steel companies. You've got to get used to buying stocks like GM, U.S. Steel, Korea Electric Power Corporation, POSCO, and Mittal Steel Company if you want to reap the rewards from this strategy.

Finally, you will face many shorter periods of time when this strategy is out of favor and styles like large-cap growth are on fire. It will take a huge amount of willpower on your part to stay the course over the short term. Do not discount the need for this fortitude should you decide to enhance your returns with individual strategies.

A Large Capitalization Growth Strategy: Market Leaders Growth

Even though my forecast for traditional large-cap growth stocks is the lowest of my estimates, I still believe you should invest a portion of your portfolio in large-cap growth stocks. Why? Because as we advance through the next twenty years, there will invariably be short periods when large-cap growth stocks are on fire, and we will want to be able to participate in those returns. Time and again my research has shown that you can do significantly better than traditional large-cap growth indexes and mutual funds if you add valuation constraints to the portfolio. One of the reasons all of those large-cap growth stocks lost more than 90 percent after the bubble was that their price valuations had hit the stratosphere. The 90 percent drop can be compared to the hangover that follows a wild night on the town. Many of the popular stocks had *no* earnings, and when they did their PE ratios often exceeded 200 times earnings. As we've learned, those types of stocks have very sexy stories, yet they inevitably come crashing back to earth. Therefore, we'll look at a large-cap growth strategy with an all-important value component in an attempt to avoid that nasty hangover.

We start with the same Market Leaders universe, but now we will add the following considerations:

1. Price-to-sales ratios must be less than the average for Market Leaders;

2. Earnings for the prior twelve-month period must exceed those of the prior year;

3. Buy the ten stocks that have the best twelve-month price appreciation.

This leads us to a selection of market-leading companies that have both earnings and price momentum, but nevertheless are still reasonably priced.

Since we are adding one year with the earnings requirement, we can only review fifty-two years of data and our rolling twenty-year real return analysis will start in 1972. For the entire period between December 31, 1952, and December 31, 2004, the ten-stock Market Leaders Growth strategy earned a real average annual return of 13.24 percent, turning one dollar invested into $641.60 at the end of 2004. The same investment in the Fama/French Large Growth Index earned a real average annual return of 6.47 percent, with one dollar growing to just $26.05. Risk was higher with the Market Leaders Growth strategy—it had a standard deviation of return of 24.42 percent compared with 18.84 percent for the Fama/French Large Growth Index. For comparative purposes, the S&P 500 returned a real average annual rate of 7.25 percent, with one dollar growing to $38.08. It also had the lowest risk of the three: 17.94 percent. Figure 8–5 graphs the returns for each of the strategies.

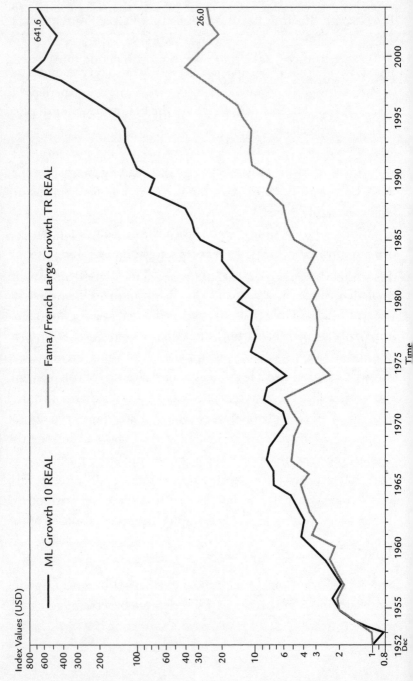

FIGURE 8–5 TERMINAL VALUE OF $1 INVESTED IN 1952

Twenty-Year Rolling Results Better than Fama/French Index and Forecast for the Next Twenty Years

The strategy's rolling twenty-year returns are also very strong. The worst return the Market Leaders Growth strategy experienced over twenty years was a real annual return of 5.39 percent per year, the best was a real annual return of 23.35 percent, and the average was 12.49 percent. The average return for all rolling twenty-year periods was 7.4 percent higher than the 5.1 percent return of the Fama/French Growth Index over the same period. This becomes our forecast for this strategy over the next twenty years. In chapter 4 I forecasted returns for traditional large-cap growth stocks through 2022–2025 between 1.97 and 3.97 percent, so I will add this strategy's average 7.4 percent premium over large-cap growth to come up with a forecast of average annual returns between 9.37 and 11.37 percent over the next twenty years. Figure 8–6 shows the rolling twenty-year returns for the strategy and the Fama/French Large Growth Index.

It is worth noting that this forecast is virtually identical to that of the large-cap value Market Leaders Low Price–to–Cash Flow strategy, perhaps because it includes a value parameter. In the next chapter we'll see that the two strategies are often out of sync with one another, with one soaring while the other swoons. Prudent asset allocation will allow us to eke even more return out of each strategy.

Small Capitalization Strategies

Now let's look at some small-cap strategies that have also significantly enhanced index returns. I'll review an extremely aggressive micro-cap strategy that looks for value stocks on the mend and a less aggressive small-cap value and growth strategy. Like our large-

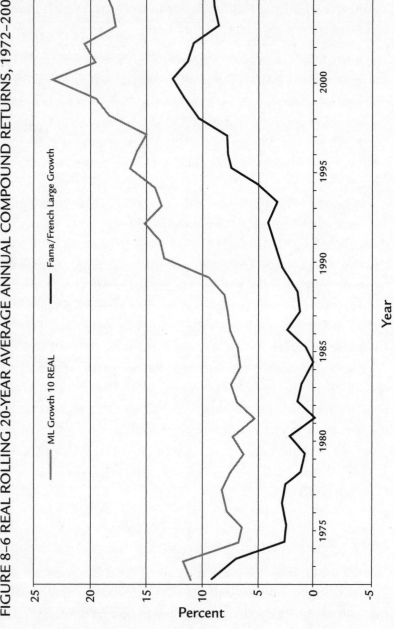

FIGURE 8-6 REAL ROLLING 20-YEAR AVERAGE ANNUAL COMPOUND RETURNS, 1972–2004

cap growth strategy, all of the small-cap growth strategies will fea-ture value carburetors to prevent us from paying too much for a stock. Also, to tame the inherent volatility of small-cap strategies, we'll need more diversification than with the large-cap variations, so here we will look at twenty-five-stock rather than ten-stock portfolios.

Tiny Titans

Tiny micro-cap stocks have several unique features that make them ideal for aggressive investors. First, as with small-cap stocks, it's virtually impossible for Wall Street analysts to give adequate coverage to micro-cap stocks. It's not worth their time to do deep research on such a large number of tiny-cap stocks. As a result, they also offer the highest upside. Second, micro-cap stocks have lower correlations with other capitalization categories. For exam-ple, while small stocks in general have an average correlation with the S&P 500 of 0.74 between 1952 and 2004, micro-caps have an even lower correlation of 0.66. This means that the performance of the S&P 500 has much less impact on micro-caps than it would on other stocks. Finally, micro-caps are extremely volatile and best suited to investors willing to accept dramatic ups and downs in their portfolios.

Let's start with the most aggressive strategy, which I call the "Tiny Titans." It buys stocks with market capitalizations between $25 million and $250 million that are both cheap and moving in price. To generate the twenty-five Tiny Titans stocks, you start with all stocks with market capitalizations between $25 million and $250 million. From this list, you remove any stocks that have a price-to-sales ratio greater than one. Finally, you buy the twenty-five stocks that have the highest twelve-month price appreciation and equally weight them. Like all of the strategies featured here, you hold them for one year and then repeat the process.

Tiny Titans is a very simple strategy that packs quite a wallop—for the fifty-three years between December 31, 1951, and December 31, 2004, the strategy had a real average annual return of 18.92 percent, turning one dollar invested in 1951 into $9,734.85 by the end of 2004! Our small-cap index offered a real average annual return of 10.44 percent per year over the same period, turning one dollar invested in 1951 into $192.85 at the end of 2004. One reason that this strategy performs so well is that you are unlikely to have heard of any of the companies it selects. I had heard of only one from the current list—Owens Corning—and that's because it used to be a big company that got sued into bankruptcy over asbestos claims. The others include Able Energy, Rural/Metro Corp., Core Molding Technologies, and the enigmatically named ENGlobal.

Before you rush out the door to put all of your money into the Tiny Titans strategy, I must emphasize the *enormous* risk that it entails. Its standard deviation of return is a whopping 38.83 percent, compared to 24.94 percent for our small stock index. That means that 95 percent of all annual returns from the strategy will fall between a *loss* of 53.04 percent and a gain of 102.28 percent! Yes, the strategy has offered awesome returns over the last fifty-three years, but you *must* ask yourself if you could realistically stomach a loss of more than half of the value of your portfolio in a single year. As I repeatedly point out in my other books, for most people the answer is no. In any event, as I'll cover in the next chapter, this strategy should only make up a small percentage of your overall portfolio. Figure 8–7 shows the returns of the strategy compared with our small-cap index.

FIGURE 8-7 TERMINAL VALUE OF $1 INVESTED IN 1951

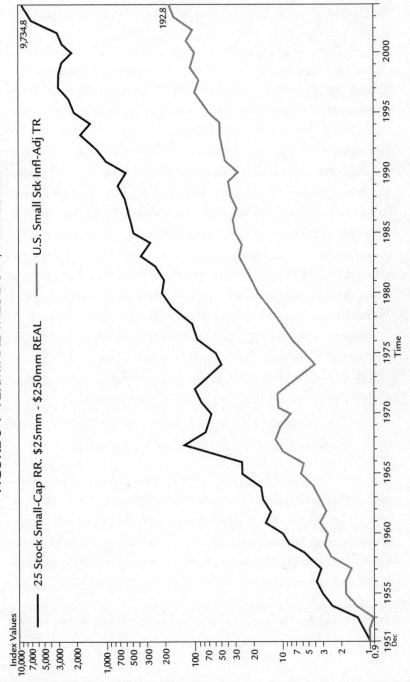

Twenty-Year Rolling Results Better Than Small Stocks Index and Forecast for the Next Twenty Years

The Tiny Titans strategy turned in some stunning numbers over all rolling twenty-year periods between 1971 and 2004—the lowest twenty-year real average annual compound return was 8.44 percent per year, the highest was 25.63 percent, and the average was 16.35 percent. In contrast, the rolling returns for our small capitalization index for the same period found a minimum return of 4.68 percent per year, a maximum return of 14.12 percent per year, and an average of 9.26 percent per year. Figure 8–8 shows the strategy's rolling twenty-year real rates of return compared with our small-cap index.

Thus, the Tiny Titans strategy outpaced standard small-cap returns by 7.09 percent per year for all rolling twenty-year periods. Since my forecast for small-cap stocks is an annual real rate of return between 7.6 and 9.6 percent over the next twenty years, the forecast for this strategy is between 14.69 percent and 16.69 percent per year through 2022–2025. Chapter 12 will cover how you can find stocks meeting these criteria should you want to put together your own portfolio.

A Small Capitalization Growth and Value Strategy

In the world of small-cap stocks, we've found that a strategy with both value and growth characteristics works very well. Here, we will be looking at the more traditional small stocks with capitalizations between $200 million and $2 billion. These stocks are less volatile than micro-caps, and offer excellent returns by combining value and growth. With this strategy, we will require that:

1. Market capitalization is between $200 million and $2 billion (inflation-adjusted) at the time of purchase;

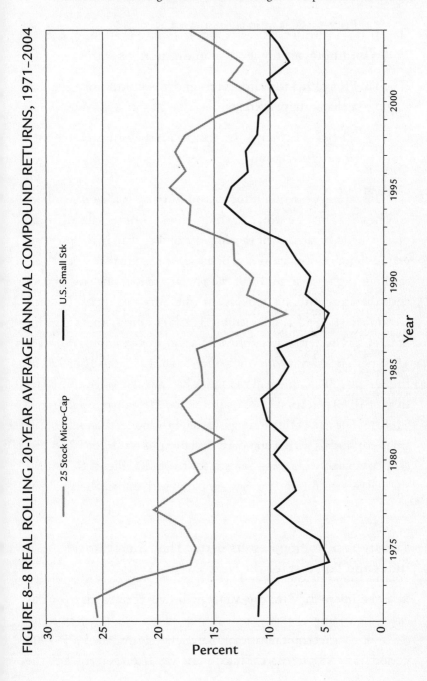

FIGURE 8-8 REAL ROLLING 20-YEAR AVERAGE ANNUAL COMPOUND RETURNS, 1971–2004

2. Price-to-sales ratio is less than 1.5;

3. Earnings are higher than in the previous year;

4. From 1963 forward, three- and six-month price appreciation is above average;

5. We buy the twenty-five stocks with the best twelve-month price appreciation.

This strategy essentially focuses on *cheap stocks on the mend.* They are cheap because we won't pay more than 1.5 times sales; they are on the mend because their earnings are higher than in the previous year and their prices are rising. Because we require that stocks have earnings higher than in the previous year, we lose one year of data and therefore will be looking at the fifty-two years between December 31, 1952, and December 31, 2004. During that time, this Small-Cap Growth strategy provided a real average annual return of 15.55 percent, turning one dollar invested in 1952 into $1,839.50 by the end of 2004. Our small-cap index had a real average annual return of 10.60 percent over the same period, turning one dollar into $188.33. The risk of this strategy was slightly higher than that of the small-cap index, with a standard deviation of return of 27.58 percent compared with 25.14 percent for the index. Figure 8-9 shows the real returns for the strategy compared with our small-cap index.

Twenty-Year Rolling Results Better Than Small Stocks Index and Forecast for the Next Twenty Years

Like the micro-cap strategy, this Small-Cap Growth strategy has excellent rolling twenty-year real rates of return. The minimum real twenty-year rate of return for the strategy during the 1972–2004 period was 7.88 percent, the maximum was 18.63 percent, and the

FIGURE 8-9 TERMINAL VALUE OF $1 INVESTED IN 1952

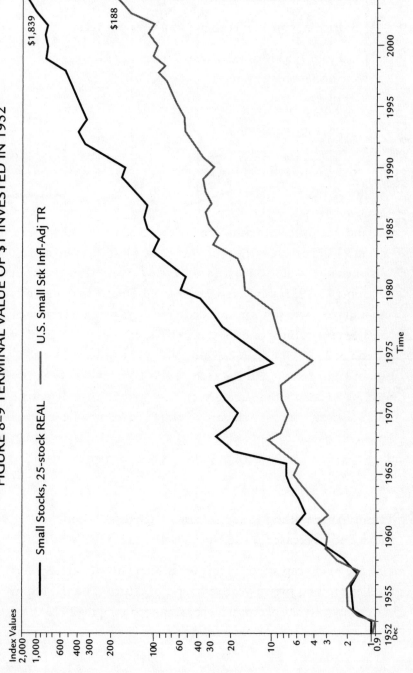

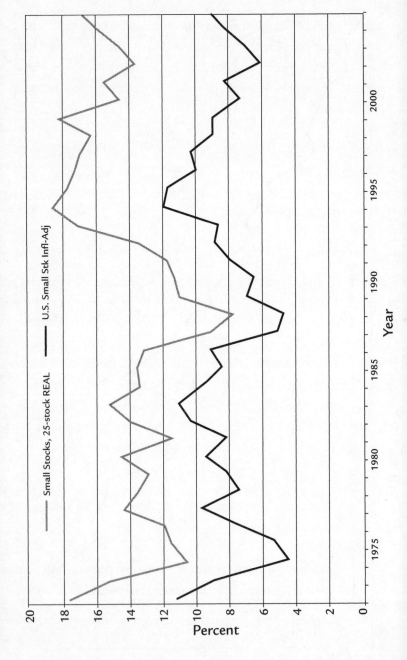

FIGURE 8-10 REAL ROLLING 20-YEAR AVERAGE ANNUAL COMPOUND RETURNS, 1972–2004

average was 14.11 percent. Over the same period the minimum real twenty-year real rate of return for the small-cap index was 4.68 percent, the maximum was 14.12 percent, and the average was 9.20 percent. Figure 8–10 shows the real rolling twenty-year rates of return of each.

Thus, for all rolling twenty-year periods, this Small-Cap Growth strategy had a performance advantage of 4.91 percent over the small-cap index. Adding this to my forecast for small-cap stocks gives us a forecasted real gain between 12.51 and 14.51 percent per year through 2022-2025.

A Less Volatile All-Cap Value Strategy with a Growth Twist

The final strategy we'll look at is a combination strategy that requires a stock to have several characteristics in common. I developed this strategy in an effort to reduce the overall variability of a portfolio's return. This All-Cap Value with a Growth Twist strategy is the first all-capitalization strategy we'll review, and is a good addition to pure-play small- to large-cap strategies. With data back to December 31, 1956, we only have forty-eight years of annual data to analyze for this strategy. Nevertheless, it demonstrates excellent performance with much lower risk than the micro-cap strategy.

We begin with all stocks in the COMPUSTAT database with market capitalizations exceeding an inflation-adjusted $200 million. That gives us a universe of liquid, easy-to-trade names. From this group, we will only consider stocks that:

1. Are in the bottom three deciles by price-to-sales ratios (the 30 percent of stocks with the lowest PSR);

2. Are in the bottom three deciles by price–to–cash flow ratio (the 30 percent of stocks with the lowest price-to–cash flow ratios);

3. Are in the top three deciles by dividend yield (the 30 percent of stocks with the highest dividend yields);

If more than twenty-five stocks make it through the first three criteria, we will then buy the twenty-five stocks with the best twelve-month price appreciation.

As with the other strategies, we will hold the names for one year, and annually rebalance the portfolio.

Between 1956 and 2004, this All-Cap Value with a Growth Twist strategy provided a real average annual return of 12.66 percent per year, turning one dollar invested on December 31, 1956, into $305 at the end of 2004. Our small-cap index provided a real average annual compound return of 10.15 percent over the same period, with one dollar growing to $103.50 over the same period. By comparison, the S&P 500 returned a real average annual return of 6.28 percent per year, with one dollar invested at the end of 1956 growing to $18.58 by the end of 2004.

What's more, this strategy took less risk than the small-cap index, providing the superior returns with a standard deviation of return of 22.14 percent, compared to 24.97 percent for the small-cap index. Thus, its risk-adjusted rate of return was dramatically higher than that for the small-cap index or the S&P 500. Figure 8–11 shows the returns for each strategy.

Twenty-Year Rolling Results Better Than S&P 500 and Forecast for the Next Twenty Years

The good news for this All-Cap Value with a Growth Twist strategy is that it never had a twenty-year period when it underperformed the S&P 500. Between 1978 and 2004, the minimum real return was 9.08 percent per year, the maximum was 15.93 percent,

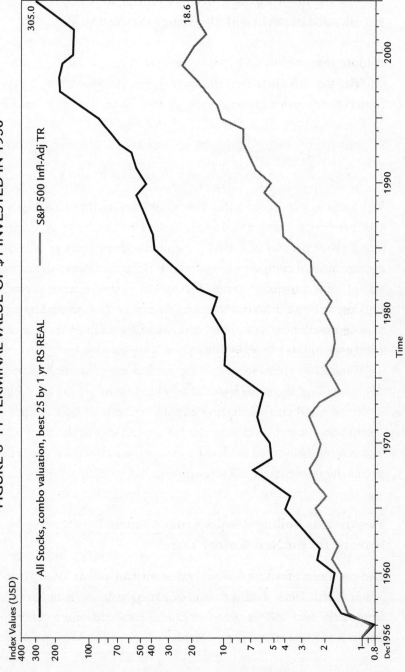

FIGURE 8–11 TERMINAL VALUE OF $1 INVESTED IN 1956

All Stocks, combo valuation, best 25 by 1 yr RS REAL

S&P 500 Infl-Adj TR

and the average was 12.31 percent. Over the same period and using annual data, the minimum return for the S&P 500 was 0.84 percent, the maximum was 13.34 percent, and the average was 6.03 percent.

Thus, adding this average advantage to my projection for the S&P 500, we arrive at a twenty-year forecasted rate of return for this strategy between 9.28 and 11.28 percent.

Using Stock Selection Strategies Instead of Indexes

The stock selection strategies covered in this chapter can significantly enhance your portfolio's returns. You must, however, understand that there will be times when any given strategy will do significantly worse than its benchmark index and other strategies. For example, I used to run the O'Shaughnessy Cornerstone Growth Fund, a mutual fund that utilized the Small-Cap Growth strategy featured in this chapter. (The fund is still available through the Hennessy Funds.) During Wall Street's speculative fever between 1996 and 2000, the fund's small-cap stocks weren't keeping up with the technology and growth stocks dominating the big-cap S&P 500.

I received many dismaying e-mails and phone calls from investors who were upset that the fund was lagging the S&P 500 and NASDAQ indexes. And while the fund *was* doing significantly better than the Russell 2000, its appropriate benchmark, investors were still disgruntled by its performance compared to that of the large-cap indexes.

The most important thing to remember with any carefully chosen investment strategy is that there will always be times when they underperform other strategies or other segments of the market. It is only those investors who can keep their focus on the very long term who will be able to reap the rewards of a long-term commitment to an intelligent strategy. Successful investors must

FIGURE 8–12 REAL ROLLING 20-YEAR AVERAGE ANNUAL COMPOUND RETURNS, 1978–2004

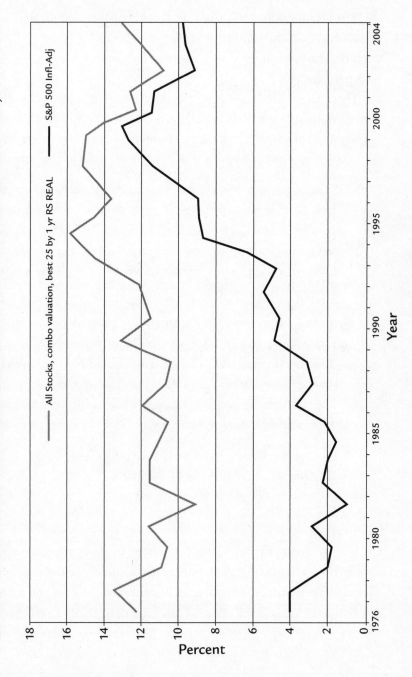

keep their guard up and resist the urge to let what the market is doing today influence their investment decisions.

Chapter Eight Highlights

◆ You can significantly improve your returns from each investment style by using stock selection strategies that have demonstrated superior returns over long periods of time.

◆ Concentrated portfolios are acceptable with large-cap strategies. With small-cap strategies, you need to own a greater number of stocks to reduce overall volatility. With the large-cap strategies, you can use ten-stock portfolios. Small-cap strategies require a minimum of twenty-five stocks to achieve adequate diversification.

◆ Growth strategies that include value parameters do much better than traditional growth stocks alone, because they exclude overvalued and overhyped stocks. Traditional growth strategies are extremely volatile because they allow very high valuation stocks to be purchased. Historically, this has led to significant underperformance.

◆ Each of the strategies covered here can be used to meet the allocations recommended in this book.

9

Using Mutual Funds and
Exchange Traded Funds

Ninety percent of what passes for brilliance or
incompetence in investing is the ebb and flow of
investment style—growth, value, small, foreign.
—Jeremy Grantham

Because most investors don't want to be bothered with
the hassles of running their own stock portfolios, mutual funds
are currently one of the most popular investment vehicles for investors. They are easy to buy and follow, allow for broad portfolio
diversification, reduce the hassles of having to conduct research,
and eliminate the need to buy and sell individual stocks in accor-
dance with a strategy. Because they are also the investment of
choice for most 401(k) plans, mutual funds remain the cornerstone of most investors' portfolios.

But mutual funds can be tricky for investors as well. With traditional mutual funds, a manager can—and often does—change a portfolio's strategy in any way that he or she sees fit. If you buy a fund to fulfill a large-cap value allocation and later discover that the manager has been buying up growth stocks, your portfolio will no longer be properly allocated, which in turn could dramatically impact your overall return.

A good example of this mutual fund pitfall is the Fidelity Magellan Fund, long heralded as one of America's premier growth funds. And while the Magellan fund has been under the management of current portfolio manager Bob Stansky, it has remained consistently focused on growth stocks. Unfortunately, that has not always been the case.

When Stansky's predecessor Jeff Vinik ran the fund, he shifted the fund's focus to large-cap *value* stocks, thinking they would perform better in the short term. Thus, while investors had expected Magellan to be a growth fund, it really looked a lot more like a large-cap value fund. Worse yet, Vinik also made a huge bet that bonds would perform well, shifting some 40 percent of the fund assets into bonds. Talk about style drift! Even if Vinik had been right about bonds—which he wasn't—he shouldn't have put bonds in a fund that was still being touted as the best growth stock fund in America. Magellan soon looked much more like a balanced *value* fund, which offers investors a more sedate mix of conservative stocks, bonds, and cash. This type of style drift is much more common than investors realize. Yet it is only excusable in mutual funds that bill themselves as all-cap, all-style investments, and is generally more appropriate for hedge funds or separately managed accounts. Therefore, if you're investing in traditional mutual funds, it's vital to keep a close eye on portfolio composition to make sure it is staying in the style category you want.

Exchange Traded Funds to the Rescue

Luckily, there is a new investment product for investors trying to build a portfolio that adheres to my recommendations for the next twenty years. Exchange traded funds, or ETFs, are similar to mutual funds in that they generally invest in broad style or capitalization categories, yet they offer several distinct advantages over traditional mutual funds.

First, because they are more like index funds, they offer greater style consistency than most mutual funds. There are ETFs for every style of investing, and one of their hallmarks is that they remain true to their stated investment objective. Thus, if you buy a Russell 2000 value ETF, you will be getting a pure play on small-cap value stocks, without a manager interceding and changing the focus of the fund.

Second, ETFs are much more tax-efficient than traditional mutual funds. Traditional mutual funds are not terribly tax-friendly for several reasons. First, if a fund has owned a high-performance stock for a long time (think of an investment made in Microsoft ten years ago) and then sells that stock, current shareholders receive the capital gain distribution, even if they just bought the fund and reaped little of the reward! This is called an embedded capital gain, and many of the most popular and successful funds have lots of them. Second, if a fund is faced with shareholder redemptions, it must sell its underlying securities to pay its departing shareholders. If these sales trigger capital gains, they are passed on to remaining shareholders, leaving *you* holding a tax bill because of the actions of *other* investors. Because of the structure of ETFs, embedded capital gains almost never occur. There still may be tax consequences since the composition of the ETF does change periodically and they pay out distributions; nevertheless, these occur far less than with traditional mutual funds.

Third, ETFs generally cost considerably less than mutual funds. Because they are structured like index funds, their fees are extremely low. For example, the expense ratio of the iShares Russell 2000 Index fund, which broadly tracks small-cap stocks, is 20 basis points (0.2 percent) annually, whereas a typical actively managed small-cap fund would have an expense ratio between 90 and 145 basis points (0.90 percent to 1.45 percent). Since these are annual charges, they can really add up over time. Last, but not least, since ETFs trade like stocks, you can build an overall asset allocation through a brokerage account.

Specifics for Capturing the Twenty-Year Trend

Clearly, if you want your portfolio to capture the trends emerging over the next twenty years, ETFs should be your first line of defense. One of the best initial investments you can make is to become a premium member of Morningstar at www.morningstar.com. The membership costs $125 per year and gives you unlimited access to all Morningstar data. They have an extensive section on ETFs that you can use to help decide which ETF is right for you. No doubt many new additional ETFs will be launched after publication of this book, so you can keep up with all innovations at Morningstar's Web site. For now, we'll look at the existing funds that best fit our needs.

Large-Cap Value ETFs

Let's look at which funds you should choose to capture the best returns, beginning with three acceptable alternatives for large-cap value. First, the iShares Russell 1000 Value Fund (Ticker IWD) replicates the well-known Russell index, holding approximately seven hundred large-cap stocks with low price-to-book ratios.

(This ETF offers returns closest to the Fama/French Large Value Index we used to generate forecasts in chapter 4, as it is constructed using a similar methodology to Fama/French.) Sponsored by the world's largest manager of indexed portfolios, Barclays Global Fund Advisors, its expense ratio is a low 20 basis points. Since this index mirrors the Fama/French index, our forecast for its returns will be the same as that for the index. The portfolio is rebalanced annually in May, so turnover remains low. Historically, large stocks with low price-to-book ratios have done much better than other large-cap stocks, and this index adequately captures those returns.

As we saw in chapter 8, you can often find strategies that significantly improve on simple index returns, and our next fund may do just that. Rather than simply using low price-to-book criteria, the Vanguard Value Vipers Fund (Ticker VTV) relies on a more sophisticated multifactor model developed by index creator MSCI. The fund ranks stocks by three value factors and five growth factors, sorting the stocks with the highest value scores into the value index and those with the highest growth scores into the growth index. The value factors MSCI relies on are price-to-book ratio; PE ratio (using forward twelve-month earnings estimates), and dividend yield. Thus, stocks selected will score well on both low price-to-book and PE, and will also have higher dividend yields. When testing similar methodologies for *What Works on Wall Street*, I found using multifactor models added to total returns, so this fund appears to be the next generation in index funds. The fund contains approximately 750 large-cap value names and is reviewed semiannually in May and November. It has an expense ratio of just 15 basis points, well below the average of 140 basis points for actively managed large-cap value funds.

The final large-cap value ETF is made up of large-cap stocks with high dividend yields. According to Morningstar, the iShares Dow Jones Select Dividend Fund (Ticker DVY) is "designed to provide exposure to liquid stocks with above-average yields and the ability to continue paying and increasing their dividends. Dow Jones screens its 1,600-member Total Market Index for 100 stocks that have three-month average daily trading volumes of 200,000 shares, have increased their dividends over the last five years, and that have paid out no more than 60% of their earnings. The index screens out REITs because they do not qualify for the dividend tax cut passed in 2003." In an attempt to assure that investors will always have exposure to higher dividend stocks, the fund will also immediately remove any stock that eliminates or substantially reduces its dividend. Unlike the first two large-value ETFs, this fund holds only one hundred stocks and is therefore more concentrated. It also has a higher expense ratio of 40 basis points, twice that of the first two entries. Its current dividend yield of 3.03 percent is higher than the S&P 500 and may provide a nice cushion in a low-return market environment. Indeed, in a backtest of similar criteria using the COMPUSTAT database, between December 31, 1969, and December 31, 2004, this type of strategy provided a real average annual compound return of 10.48 percent per year, compared to just 6.25 percent per year for the S&P 500. The two had similar risk levels, with the high dividend strategy sporting a standard deviation of return of 17.80 percent and the S&P 500 16.88 percent. For the period for which we have Russell data, December 31, 1979, through December 31, 2004, the high dividend strategy did better than the Russell 1000 Value Index, returning a real average annual compound return of 14.49 percent per year versus 10.15 percent per year for the Russell 1000 Value Index, also with similar risk levels. All told, this could be an excellent large-cap value choice for your portfolio.

Large-Cap Growth

Because many of the large-cap growth ETFs use simple price-to-book methodologies to distinguish between value and growth stocks—with high price-to-book stocks assigned to the growth index—I do not recommend them. As we've seen in earlier chapters, I expect high price-to-book stocks to do horribly over the next twenty years. What's more, a high price-to-book value does not make a growth stock.

However, one growth ETF does bear examination: the Vanguard Growth Viper Fund (Ticker VUG). Like its value counterpart, this fund is designed to track the MSCI Prime Market Growth Index, which is made up of the 750 highest-scoring stocks from a multifactor growth model developed by MSCI. While all stocks are ranked on eight factors, those in the MSCI Prime Market Growth Index score the highest on the following five variables:

1. Long-term forward earnings per share growth rate;

2. Short-term forward earnings per share growth rate;

3. Current internal growth rate;

4. Long-term historical earnings per share growth trend; and

5. Long-term historical sales per share growth trend.

Thus, stocks in the index must have excellent forecasted and historic earnings and sales growth, rather than just a high price-to-book ratio. This is a far more refined method for building a portfolio of large-cap stocks with great growth characteristics and is far more consistent with growth models that have performed well historically. If you are planning to build a portfolio exclusively using ETFs, the Vanguard Growth Viper Fund is worth considering, particularly in light of its rock-bottom 15 basis point expense ratio. However, I do believe that when it comes to the large-cap growth component of your portfolio, you will be better off choosing an actively managed fund that scores well on both growth and value characteristics. I'll cover this in detail later in this chapter.

Small-Cap ETF Choices

The best ETF for broad exposure to small-cap stocks is the iShares Russell 2000 Fund (Ticker IWM), which is designed to track the performance of the two thousand smallest companies in the Russell 3000 Index. Managed by Barclays Global Fund Advisors, the world's largest manager of indexed portfolios, the fund's expense ratio is 20 basis points, well below the average for actively managed small-cap funds. It is the ideal choice for a broad investment in small-cap stocks.

Your choices are more limited if you want separate ETFs by small-cap growth and small-cap value. A good choice for small-cap value is the iShares Russell 2000 Value Fund (Ticker IWN). This fund tracks the Russell 2000 Value Index, which is a subset of the Russell 2000 Index. The Value Index measures the performance of companies whose shares have lower price-to-book ratios and lower consensus forecasted growth. The fund's advisor, Barclays Global Fund Advisors, uses representative sampling to track the index. It holds nearly 1,300 stocks. The index is rebalanced once a year in May. There are data for all three Russell small-cap indexes back to December 31, 1978, giving us a good sense of how much the Russell 2000 Value Index adds to returns.

For the twenty-six years between 1978 and 2004, the Russell 2000 Value Index had a real average annual return of 11.57 percent per year, significantly ahead of the 9.07 percent real annual return earned by the non–style specific Russell 2000. It also vastly outpaced the 6.15 percent real annual return of the Russell 2000 Growth Index, and it earned this superior return with less risk: the Russell 2000 Value Index had a standard deviation of return of 18.67 percent over the period, compared with 21.87 percent for the Russell 2000 and 26.19 percent for the Russell 2000 Growth Index. Thus, you might want to use a mix of the non–style specific Russell 2000 and the Russell 2000 Value Index for your small-cap allocations.

Innovation in the ETF Market

There are several new companies devoted to the creation of new, smarter index funds using more in-depth methodologies and multifactor models. One company, Powershares LLC, has launched a host of ETFs to replicate their Intellidexes[SM], which utilize ten independent style determinants to provide comprehensive and precise style segregation. They hope that this research will give investors access to accurate, stylistically pure market exposures. Unfortunately, their Web site (www.powershares.com) is unclear about the specific methodology used to select the securities. Only time will tell whether these "smart indexes" will offer higher sustainable returns than the simple indexes already discussed.

Another firm, Index Development Partners, is also planning to issue ETFs based on quantitative models. I believe that the ETF market will continue to evolve, becoming more reliant on time-tested strategies like those featured in *What Works on Wall Street*. As they grow in sophistication, they will likely become the new investment vehicle of choice for financial professionals and individual investors alike.

Bond ETFs

You can also use ETFs to fulfill bond allocations in your portfolio. Recall that our long-term forecast favors shorter duration bonds. There are currently two ETFs in this category, both managed by Barclays. The first, iShares Lehman 1–3 Year Treasury Bond Fund (Ticker SHY), tracks the returns and yields of the Lehman Brothers U.S. Treasury: 1–3 Year Index. The index includes bonds that are less than three years old, have at least one year until maturity, have at least $250 million in par outstanding, and must be a U.S. Treasury security. It would be an excellent choice when interest rates are heading higher. For slightly longer-term bonds, there is the iShares Lehman 7–10 Year Treasury Bond Fund (Ticker IEF), which tracks the returns and yields of the Lehman Brothers 7–10 Year Treasury Bond Index. Both funds have a very low expense ratio of 15 basis points.

Finally, if rates move substantially higher and you want to lock in an inflation-protected return, take a look at the iShares Lehman TIPS Bond Fund (Ticker TIP). The fund is designed to track the Lehman Brothers U.S. Treasury Inflation Notes Index, which measures the performance of the inflation-protected public obligations of the U.S. Treasury.

Analyzing Actively Managed Funds

While ETFs should serve as key components of a style-diversified portfolio, it may be worthwhile investing in actively managed funds in the large-cap growth arena. As of this writing, large-cap growth ETFs have lagged their value brethren in sophistication. Historically, the best performing growth strategies I've found all include some value component that removes toxic, overvalued stocks from the strategy.

Here, go to Morningstar at www.morningstar.com to search for funds with good growth and value characteristics. Select the Funds category, then go to the mutual fund screener and select the category—in this instance, Large Growth—then screen for funds with an above average rating in the risk-adjusted category and five-year returns exceeding the average for the category. You'll end up with a group of funds to choose from that have good risk-adjusted returns and that have nevertheless outperformed the average large-cap growth fund covered by Morningstar.

From here, we'll need to review each fund individually. First, review the *Risk Measures* section of the report, looking for funds with low standard deviation of return and high Sharpe ratios. After removing any with poor risk statistics, go to the *Portfolio* section of the report. Look for funds that have above-average growth in historical earnings and cash flow growth, while at the same time having *lower* PE, price-to-sales, and price-to-book ratios than other funds in the category. This will lead you to a fund with a "growth at a reasonable price" philosophy, which has been documented to provide the most consistent returns in the large-cap growth category. Try to focus on funds that show no deviation from their underlying style and where there has been little turnover in the portfolio management team. That way, you'll have a fund that is more likely to remain true to its stated goals.

Putting It All Together

In chapter 12 we'll see that whether you are a do-it-yourself investor or working with an advisor, ETFs can be a good way to invest in the various style categories that I advocate in this book. Used in concert with individual strategies that have historically outperformed simple style indexes, ETFs can be used as the cornerstone in a portfolio that is well diversified between both style and capitalization. They have better style consistency, are more tax-friendly, and have lower costs than traditional mutual funds. The only exception is in the large-cap growth category, where ETFs tend to use antiquated simple selection factors like price-to-book to identify growth stocks. Remember that high price-to-book ratio stocks are rotten performers over the long term, so a multifactor approach is essential in the large-cap growth category. No doubt there will be many innovations in years to come, enabling us to cover all style categories with exchange traded funds.

Chapter Nine Highlights

◆ Mutual funds are often the best way to achieve broad diversification within an investment style. Traditionally managed funds can offer good value, provided their managers adhere to their stated style. Unfortunately, managers do occasionally abandon their underlying style. This is known as style drift.

◆ Exchange traded funds (ETFs) are mutual funds that trade like stocks. They follow a disciplined, index-like approach and cover every major capitalization and style category. They are more tax-friendly than traditional mutual funds and tend to have lower total expenses than mutual funds.

◆ There are three acceptable ETFs to choose from in the large-cap value category and two in the small-cap category. I do not currently recommend any large-cap growth ETFs, with the possible exception of the Vanguard Growth Viper Fund. For this portion of your portfolio allocation, I suggest you look at a traditionally managed large-cap growth fund with a "growth at a reasonable price" methodology.

10

401(k)s: Tax-Advantaged Savings Work

> Eighty percent of success is showing up.
>
> —Woody Allen

A journey of a thousand miles begins with a single step. And so it is with your retirement planning. 401(k) plans are a fabulous way to save and invest for your future, but far too many investors delay that all-important first step—setting up and contributing annually to a 401(k) plan. The impact that tax-deferred 401(k) contributions can have on your net worth is nothing short of amazing. By maximizing the amount of your tax-free or tax-deferred investments you also maximize the final value of your portfolio.

The Tax Man Cometh

The bite that taxes take out of the terminal value of your portfolio can be enormous. Yet, much like with the effects of inflation, few of us consider what a huge negative impact taxes have on our wealth. In chapter 2 we saw that one dollar invested in 1927 grew to $187 at the end of 2004, a real return of 6.98 percent. But a major part of that growth is due to the effects of compounding, allowing you to earn money on prior gains. When Uncle Sam extracts his pound of flesh, you have less capital available for reinvestment. The effects of a 28 percent capital gains tax are staggering. At that 6.98 percent growth rate, one dollar invested in the S&P 500 grew to $187 by the end of 2004. If you had been forced to pay an average annual capital gains tax of 28 percent, that same dollar would be worth a mere $34.89 at the end of 2004! (This assumes that you harvest losses to offset income during times when the market is providing losses.) Taxes would have wiped out the vast majority of your gain. What's more, the actual capital gain tax rate over those years was variable, but generally much *higher* than the 28 percent assumed in this example. Keep in mind that you're also taxed on *nominal* gains, meaning that during inflationary times the bite of the tax man is unusually large.

Clearly, it's vital to maximize your tax-free investments. This means that if you have a 401(k) plan, you should make the largest contribution to it possible, or set up an IRA or Keogh account. Yet investors are hardly rushing into these tax-advantaged accounts: According to *BusinessWeek*'s June 6, 2005, issue, "only about half of American workers participate in 401(k) and other employer-based retirement savings plans." Worse, the magazine adds that "fewer than 10% of eligible workers contribute the allowable maximum to 401(k) plans; more than half fail to diversify, especially beyond their employers' stock; few rebalance portfolios in response to age or market returns; and almost half withdraw from 401(k) plans when they change jobs."

Getting Started

Let's look at how you can invest in your 401(k) plan. More than 95 percent of U.S. companies with over five thousand employees currently offer a 401(k) plan to their employees, and smaller companies are adding them in droves. The catchy name, 401(k), comes from the section of the Internal Revenue Code that defines the plans. Offering special tax advantages, 401(k)s were established by the federal government in 1981 to encourage people to prepare for retirement. Essentially, 401(k)s are defined contribution plans.

IRS regulations define what you can contribute to your 401(k), but say nothing about how much it will be worth when you retire. That sum is up to you, and *will be determined by the investment choices you make*. With 401(k) plans, you make a defined contribution from your salary. The government regulates the amount that you can contribute—in 2006, the maximum contribution amount will be $15,000 as provided by the Economic Growth and Tax Relief Reconciliation Act of 2001. After 2006, these contribution limits will be increased in $500 increments to factor in the effects of inflation. It's important to remember your company's plan may have additional limits.

401(k) Retirement Plans Have Many Benefits

What makes 401(k) plans great is that your contributions are in *pretax* dollars. If you make $100,000 a year and contribute 10 percent to your 401 (k) plan, that $10,000 contribution is treated as deferred compensation, and not subject to taxes other than Social Security. As a result, when tax time comes, you'll only be taxed on an income of $90,000, your salary less your 401(k) contribution. *Every dollar you put into your 401(k) is deducted from your income taxes for that year.* If you're in the 28 percent tax bracket, it's like earning 28 percent on every dollar you put in your 401(k). That's a huge initial return on investment!

Another 401(k) benefit is that all the money you put in your 401(k) plan compounds on a tax-deferred basis. Never forget that taxes and inflation are the enemies of investment success. Granted, you'll have to pay taxes on your 401(k) savings when you start taking it out of your account—presumably when you retire. In some instances, if your planning is poor or you've done *too well* with your investments, the tax hit could be considerable. But that's a nice problem to have. Clearly, the power of compounding your money without the tax man taking his cut is overwhelming. I highly recommend IRA contributions for the same reason—even though they're not always tax deductible, they too compound on a tax-deferred basis, which enhances your returns considerably.

There's yet another reason to take advantage of your 401(k) plan. In many cases, your employer will match a portion of your 401(k) contribution, typically fifty cents for every dollar you contribute. To use our example above, your $10,000 contribution would be matched by a $5,000 contribution from your employer. That's like getting an instant 50 percent return on your investment! If you work for a company that matches a portion of your 401(k) contribution, you'd be foolish to pass it up.

Finally, 401(k) plans are today's retirement plan of choice because they're portable and follow you from job to job. All your contributions are yours alone, and, after your contributions become vested—typically after a certain number of years with your company—all of the money your employer contributed is yours as well. All together, 401(k) plans are a great way to maximize your after-tax wealth.

The Basics

Now let's learn about your 401(k) and look at the best ways to invest the money you put in it. The government allows your employer to restrict who gets to participate in their 401(k) plan, but the restrictions are usually not onerous. The most important eligibility standards are simple: your employer can prohibit you from joining until you've been with the company for a year or until you are twenty-one. Your employer may not offer a 401(k) plan to all employees. If you work for a big company, for example, only certain employees or certain divisions may be eligible. While there are fewer restrictions today than in the past, they can still be a problem. If you *don't* have a 401(k) plan available to you or your company offers another type of pension plan, it's important to learn as much as you can about what your company is offering.

Your Company's 401(k) Plan

The first thing to do is get the specifics on your company's plan. Don't be surprised if your personnel manager or human resources manager gives you a blank stare when you ask about it, as it's not unusual for 401(k)s to be delegated to a plan administrator. Depending on the size of your company, the *plan administrator* is either someone within the human resources department or a person from an outside firm that specializes in plan administration.

Who Does What?

The *plan sponsor* is your employer, or the company offering the plan. They define the structure of the plan, what investments are available, how you can invest your money, and finally, whether they are going to match a portion of the money you contribute.

The *trustee* of the 401(k) plan is either an individual or committee that has overall responsibility for the plan. They report to the plan sponsor. The *plan administrator* is the person or outside company that provides you all the information you'll need to get your 401(k) started. The *investment managers* are usually outside firms that offer mutual funds or money management services. They are the ones who actually buy and sell securities, bonds, or Treasury bills on your behalf. Finally, the *record keeper* is just that. It is usually an outside firm that keeps track of all the paperwork, contributions, investments, and other information having to do with the plan and its participants.

When you inquire about your firm's 401(k), you'll usually receive a *summary plan description* that tells you what your company's plan provides and how it operates. It will outline your investment choices, from investing in outside mutual funds to purchasing company stock. It explains such things as when you can start participating, how to contact the plan administrator, and how to make contributions. Hardly thrilling reading—but the summary plan description will give you the nuts and bolts description of your company's 401(k) plan. The *summary annual report* summarizes the financial reports that the plan files with the Department of Labor.

The *individual benefit statement* is more interesting. That's the document that describes how much money you've accrued and what percentages of your benefits are vested. It's essentially a summary detailing how much money you have in your retirement account. The *material modifications document* is a summary of any changes in your company's plan. If they change the plan by adding or dropping a mutual fund or making a new asset class available to you, you will learn about it in this report.

Where to Invest Your 401(k)

Okay, let's say you're contributing the most that you can to your 401(k), and you're taking full advantage of every matching benefit that your employer offers—now what do you do? While we will cover overall portfolio allocations fully in the next chapter, we'll also look at some specific examples here. For all the examples I'll outline shortly, I will assume that you are forty-five years old and already have $81,000 in your 401(k). (I use these figures because the global consulting firm Hewitt Associates found this was the average-sized 401(k) account for people in their forties. Hewitt arrived at this average after studying roughly 2.5 million workers eligible to participate in the retirement plans offered by large companies.) In my calculations I will also assume that you can contribute $10,000 of your pretax income to your plan. When feasible I always advise maximizing your 401(k) contributions, but here I will take the middle road and assume the more modest $10,000 contribution.

T-bills and Bonds Offer Little

An investment in T-bills and bonds will earn very modest returns over the long term. I recommend them only to reduce your overall portfolio's volatility or when you need a reliable income *after* you've retired. As we saw in chapter 6, T-bills or money market funds are likely to do little more than keep pace with inflation, limiting your portfolio's terminal value to roughly the same amount—in real dollars—to what you've contributed to your 401(k) plan over the years. Clearly, this is not the way to maximize your total returns.

Let's look at the sad reality of investing your 401(k) in bonds or T-bills. Using the current yield on the twenty-year Treasury Inflation Protected bond of 1.79 percent as a proxy, a forty-five-year-old making annual contributions of $10,000 and earning the real return of 1.79 percent per year would have just $353,459 in his or her 401(k) at age sixty-five. That sum doesn't even get you close to a comfortable retirement, particularly if you're hoping to live off the proceeds from your portfolio. Investing your entire 401(k) in bonds would force you to either continue working past the age of sixty-five or begin consuming your portfolio's principal to support yourself.

T-bill returns are even worse. If you managed to earn the average real return from T-bills seen over all rolling twenty-year periods of 0.13 percent, your portfolio would be worth just $285,622 when you hit age sixty-five. Ouch!

Equity Allocations

Clearly, your prospects are quite bleak if you try to build your retirement nest egg with fixed income. As we saw in chapter 6, over the next several decades we're moving from a period of risk-free returns to one of return-free risks in the fixed income markets.

To take advantage of the trends I expect to unfold over the next twenty years, you'll want to find index funds, ETFs, or mutual funds available in your 401(k) plan that invest in small stocks, value stocks, and growth stocks where the fund employs a "growth at a reasonable price" philosophy.

Many 401(k) plans have added index funds and exchange traded funds to their menus. If your plan has, they should be the first place to look when allocating your portfolio. When planning for your retirement, you have three basic choices—aggressive, moderate, and conservative. While I'll give you an overall portfolio allocation process in the next chapter, you may want to use your 401(k) even more aggressively, because you aren't taxed on your portfolio's gains. Remember to balance out your 401(k) strategy with other investments outside of the plan. If you want to be aggressive, you'll want to invest the majority of your portfolio in in-dexes like the Russell 2000, the Russell 2000 Value, and the Russell 1000 Value. For the large-cap growth portion of your portfolio, remember that I do not recommend using an index, since those are typically composed of stocks with high price-to-book ratios. A moderate equity allocation for your 401(k) would be approxi-mately 50 percent of the portfolio in a large-cap value index like the Russell 1000 Value Index, 35 percent in the Russell 2000 Index (which invests in small-cap core companies), and the remaining 15 percent in a large-cap growth mutual fund using a growth-at-a-reasonable-price methodology. Finally, a conservative mix would put approximately 50 percent in large-cap value, 25 percent in small-cap, and 25 percent in a large-cap growth mutual fund us-ing a growth-at-a-reasonable-price methodology.

Instead of using an ETF or index fund for your large-cap growth allocation, you'll need to wade through the Morningstar data covering the large-cap growth mutual funds offered by your plan. (I know, you would probably rather get a root canal, but this is your future we're talking about!) As we saw in the mutual fund section, this is accomplished most easily by visiting Morningstar's Web site at www.morningstar.com. Look at the characteristics of each of your plan's large-cap growth funds and select the one that has the lowest PE and price-to-sales ratios and where the manager's style reflects a "growth at a reasonable price" philosophy. As we did in chapter 9, start with the *Risk Measures* section of the Web site. Look for large-cap growth funds with relatively low standard devi-ations and high Sharpe ratios. Next, go to the portfolio section and throw out any funds with very high price-to-book, price-to-sales, or PE ratios. Finally, focus on the large-cap growth funds that have low valuations but also show high earnings growth and strong price momentum. You should end up with funds that possess characteristics similar to the best growth strategies I uncovered in my research for *What Works on Wall Street,* and a sound investment strategy for the large-cap growth portion of your portfolio.

What About My Company's Stock?

There's a one word answer to *that* question: Enron.

More than eleven thousand Enron employees had an average of 58 percent of their 401(k) money invested in the company's stock. Their sad fate was widely reported in the news, and is an important lesson for all of us.

More generally, in plans that match employee contributions with company stock, participants hold an average of 40 percent of their assets in company stock, according to the Profit Sharing/401(k) Council of America in Chicago. Many 401(k) plans let you invest in your company's stock. I strongly discourage you from making a large investment in a single stock, however secure you think it is or however proud you may be of the company you work for. Typically, people feel it's the loyal thing to do and will put too much of their 401(k) savings in their company's stock. Indeed, in many 401(k) accounts, the company's stock accounts for 50 percent of the equity allocation! This is a huge mistake. You never want to take the exponential risk that is associated with investing in a single stock. And if you think that Enron was an anomaly because the management committed outright fraud, think of how an IBM employee who diligently invested all her money in IBM stock must have felt as she watched its price drop 50 percent in the early 1990s!

There are only two reasons you might want to invest a small percentage of your 401(k) in your company's stock. First, if the company is selling it to you at a reduced price, or second, if the stock meets the criteria of a successful time-tested strategy. Take a look at your company stock's underlying factors. Is it a market-leading company with a high dividend yield? If so, it would fit into one of the large-cap value strategies we analyzed in chapter 8. And remember, even if your company's stock does fit into a successful time-tested strategy, you should never invest more than a small percentage of your portfolio in a single stock.

It's Time to Get Going

If you have a 401(k) plan available to you and haven't yet put any money into it, *start doing so right now.* If you're forty-five years old and don't want to work until you're eighty, you've got to begin to maximize your contributions to your 401(k) immediately. Get your 401(k) set up today and start taking advantage of the tax savings it offers you. Get involved as well. If your plan has rotten investment choices, lobby your company or plan administrator to add better ones. Finally, decide on a portfolio allocation you can stick with through thick and thin. If you're risk-tolerant and aggressive, you'll want to have 40 percent in small-cap funds and indexes, 40 percent in large-cap value funds or large-cap funds of stocks paying high dividends, and 20 percent in large-cap growth funds like those outlined in this chapter.

Chapter Ten Highlights

◆ You should always take advantage of tax-deferred investment vehicles like 401(k) plans, since they can make a huge difference in the terminal value of your portfolio. One dollar invested in 1927 grows to $187 at the end of 2004 without taxes. With a 28 percent average annual capital gains tax, the same one-dollar investment grows to only $34.89.

◆ The majority of Americans do not take full advantage of their 401(k) retirement plans. They put off setting up their accounts, fail to maximize their contributions, cash out when changing jobs, and invest too heavily in their company's stock, bonds, and T-bills.

◆ You can use my recommended asset allocations for the next twenty years in your 401(k) by investing in mutual funds or ETFs. You should always elect for broadly diversified funds over single stock investments.

◆ If ETFs are available, use them. If not, analyze the underlying factors of the funds available to you by going to www.morningstar.com. Make certain that each of the funds you choose conforms to the specifications outlined here and in the mutual fund chapter.

◆ If you have not started contributing to your 401(k), start today.

11

Allocating Your Assets: The Best Portfolios for the Next Twenty Years

> To be conscious that you are ignorant is a great step to knowledge.
>
> —Benjamin Disraeli

It is now time for us to put our new knowledge to work. How you allocate your portfolio can make a *material* difference to your total future returns. We've analyzed both the trends that will likely unfold over the next twenty years and the types of investment vehicles available; let's now build portfolios that take maximum advantage of each. In this chapter I'll show you how to use the allocations in any account, be it a 401(k), IRA, or regular brokerage account. I'll also explain how you can use the stock selection strategies from chapter 8 to build a custom portfolio. You can also work with your advisor to use the suggested allocations as a framework for your equity portfolio allocations. Remember that a good advisor may offer additional investments like foreign equities, commodities, and hedge funds that will enable you to further diversify your portfolio and enhance returns over the next twenty years.

We'll first look at what your portfolio might be worth if you simply leave it invested in a classic mix of large-cap core stocks (like the S&P 500) and large-cap growth stocks (still the dominant holding for many investors), thereby ignoring the trends I believe will unfold over the next two decades. We'll then look at two separate allocations designed to maximize returns over the next twenty years, one for more conservative investors and one for more aggressive investors seeking to maximize their returns. I will refer to this more aggressive portfolio as the preferred allocation, as it is the one that I believe takes the fullest advantage of the trends identified in this book. Finally, we'll see how much better you can do if you use the stock selection strategies featured in chapter 8, and how simple changes in asset allocation can affect your portfolio.

Assumptions

For the sake of clarity, I will make some simplifying assumptions here. First, I assume a steady-state forecasted return over the next twenty years. While this is certainly not what will happen, it is the best way to analyze portfolios over the long term. In reality, returns are quite variable over time. You will see style and capitalization groups move in and out of favor, and those short-term gyrations will test your mettle. I'm also quite certain that at some point in the next twenty years, the allocations and strategies I recommend here will be near the *bottom* of the pack over shorter periods of time. Never underestimate the regret you will feel in times like these or the strength of will that staying the course will require.

Second, I'll be looking at gross returns, not returns net of fees and taxes. Since taxes and fees will be different for everyone, there is no truly accurate way for me to take them into account in this discussion. That does not mean taxes and fees aren't very important factors to consider—they are. As we saw in chapter 10, taxes can wreak havoc on your portfolio's final value, so if you are using a taxable account, you should adjust your expectations accordingly. You should also try to take long-term rather than short-term gains, as they are taxed at a far lower rate. All of the stock selection strategies featured in chapter 8 use a one-year holding period, but if you sell a holding after one year plus one day, it will be considered a long-term gain. I also exclude management fees in this gross return analysis. Obviously, if you are a do-it-yourselfer you are going to pay lower fees than someone working with an advisor; in either case you'll want to adjust the gross returns featured here to reflect your own situation. Keep in mind that if you are using traditional mutual funds, you should deduct the fund's expense ratio from your expected return, just as you should deduct any advisor fee. Many advisors and mutual funds now show pro forma analysis net of fees—ask for it.

Finally, I'll be looking at the returns to a lump-sum investment of $100,000. Obviously, this is not the way that a majority of investments are made, and it will tend to understate the returns you might actually earn. This is because a lump-sum calculation does not take any ongoing contributions into account. If you are using a 401(k) or IRA you will in all likelihood be making yearly investments, typically buying less when stock prices are high and more when they are low (the central tenet of dollar cost averaging). Nor does the lump sum calculation reflect the advantages of cash flow into your portfolio when the time comes to rebalance. The brilliance of rebalancing is that it forces you to take money *away* from the previous year's strongest performing asset classes and put money into those that have performed the worst. This enforces a buy-low, sell-high methodology which is actually intensified when you continually add money to your portfolio. I will give an example of this effect later in this chapter.

Equity Allocations

Let's first look at portfolios that are just invested in stocks. Since I believe that stocks will outperform bonds over the next twenty years—even with the lower forecasts for certain equity sectors—you should invest the bulk of your portfolio in equities to maximize your returns. Later in this chapter we'll look at when you should include bonds, which may become more attractive investments if bond yields rise in years to come.

A Conventional Allocation

For the first allocation, let's look at a portfolio rooted in traditional allocations of the past. It will invest 50 percent in large-cap core stocks (we'll use the S&P 500 as a proxy), 40 percent in large-cap growth stocks, and 10 percent in small-cap stocks. We'll rebalance the portfolio annually to keep this mix constant. Figure 11–1 shows the constant balance the portfolio will hold over the period.

Between June 30, 1927, and December 31, 2004, a portfolio with this 50-40-10 mix would have earned a real annual return of 7.09 percent, with an overall standard deviation of 21.71 percent. One dollar invested in this portfolio in 1927 would have been worth $201.45 at the end of 2004. From a rolling twenty-year perspective, the lowest twenty-year real return this allocation ever ex-

FIGURE 11–1 TRADITIONAL EQUITY ASSET ALLOCATION

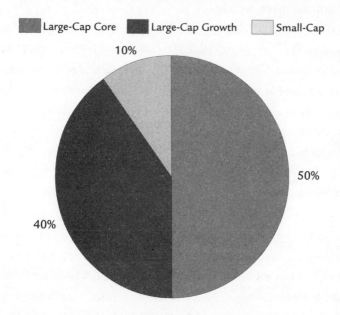

perienced was a real gain of 0.89 percent per year; the highest was 14.03 percent and the average was 7.36 percent.

Let's now look at how this allocation is likely to perform over the next twenty years. Remember that our forecasted real return for the S&P 500 (core large-cap equities) is a mere 3 to 5 percent, for large-cap growth it is 1.97 to 3.97 percent, and for small-cap stocks it is 7.62 to 9.62 percent. Given these expectations, let's look at what might happen. If this traditionally allocated portfolio achieved returns in line with our minimum expectations, it would be worth $182,373 in twenty years (in 2005 dollars) but worth $267,868 if returns came in at the high end of expectations. That's a real annual return of between 3.05 and 5.05 percent for the portfolio. Notice that this return is nearly the same as a portfolio that was 100 percent invested in the S&P 500. That's because the 10 percent allocation to the higher-returning small-cap stocks is not large enough to make a meaningful difference to the portfolio's overall performance.

Remember that this 50-40-10 allocation is a classic portfolio that millions of investors currently use to save for their retirement or other goals. I think that many of these investors would be shocked to learn of their portfolio's limited potential over the next twenty years. If you're forty-five years old and have $100,000 in your 401(k) invested in a similar fashion, it is sobering indeed to think that in twenty years you will have only earned $82,000. Let this serve as a wake-up call and an incentive to choose a better allocation for the future.

The Conservative Portfolio Allocation

If my arguments about mean-reversion and where the markets are headed have convinced you, but you still worry about the volatility of the more promising small-cap stocks, you can still take advantage of the twenty-year trends by moving 25 percent of your portfolio to small-cap stocks and 75 percent to large-cap names. This is the more conservative path. The difference between the conservative and preferred portfolio allocations is the percentage invested in small-cap stocks. While they have the highest expected rate of return over the next twenty years, they also have the highest volatility. This means that along with a larger allocation to small-cap stocks comes increased risk and increased potential reward. Note that with both the conservative and preferred portfolio allocations, I limit the large-cap growth exposure to 15 percent, with 60 percent of the large-cap allocation going to value stocks. Recall that I expect large-cap growth to underperform in the coming two decades. It is, however, prone to short bursts of strong performance, so a 15 percent allocation is high enough to have a meaningful impact on a portfolio when large-cap growth is in favor, yet small enough to prevent any significant drag on performance.

For the conservative portfolio allocation, we will take advantage of the higher expected returns from large-cap value stocks rather than the more volatile small-caps. The conservative portfolio mix is 25 percent small-cap stocks, 60 percent large-cap value stocks and 15 percent large-cap growth stocks. Figure 11–2 shows the allocation. As before, we'll annually rebalance the portfolio to maintain these percentages. Historically, this mix earned a real annual return of 8.77 percent between 1927 and 2004. Over this period, one dollar invested grew to $673.12, with a fairly high standard deviation of return of 27.72 percent. From the perspective of rolling twenty-year returns, the worst twenty-year period for this conservative allocation was a real annual return of 2.50

FIGURE 11–2 CONSERVATIVE ALLOCATION

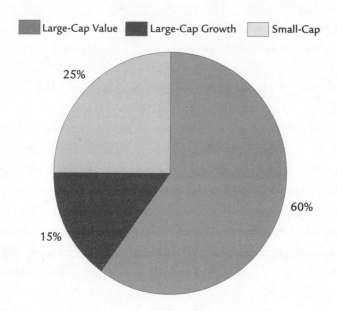

percent; the best was 16.33 percent and the average 9.97 percent. Reviewing our twenty-year forecasts for each category, we see that large-cap value stocks should earn between 6.03 and 8.03 percent, large-cap growth stocks between 1.97 and 3.97 percent, and small-cap stocks between 7.62 and 9.62 percent.

By using these forecasted returns, we see that this conservative mix offers a much improved expected return over the next twenty years. Should we earn returns consistent with the minimum expected forecasted returns, the $100,000 lump-sum portfolio would be worth $310,911 (in 2005 dollars) in twenty years' time, a real annual return of 5.84 percent. If we earned returns at the maximum expected returns, the portfolio would be worth $452,109, a real annual return of 7.84 percent, some 60 basis points higher than the S&P 500's twenty-year rolling returns over the last seventy-five years. When we get to the allocations using specific stock selection strategies, we'll see that you can earn even higher returns with lower volatility. The important lesson here is that with this conservative mix of mostly large-cap value stocks, you can expect to earn a return slightly higher than that of the S&P 500 in all rolling twenty-year periods.

The Preferred Portfolio Allocation

The only difference between the conservative and preferred allocations is the percentage of small-cap stocks in the portfolio, now with a 35 percent rather than a 25 percent allocation. We will lower the large-cap value stocks' allocation to 50 percent and maintain the 15 percent large-cap growth allocation. Figure 11–3 details the portfolio allocation. This 10 percent increase in small-caps has a good effect on performance. Historically, this allocation offered a real annual return of 9.11 percent, turning one dollar invested in 1927 into $860.04 at the end of 2004. Its volatility is slightly higher than that of the conservative allocation, with a standard deviation of 28.90 percent. From the perspective of rolling twenty-year returns, the worst twenty-year return was 3.26 percent; the highest was 16.65 percent and the average return for all twenty-year periods was 10.15 percent.

Let's look at the potential of this preferred portfolio allocation, using the same forecasts as with the conservative allocation. If returns come in at our minimum expectations, this $100,000 preferred portfolio would grow to $320,215 in twenty years, a real annual return of 5.99 percent. With returns at the maximum of our expected forecasts, the portfolio would be worth $465,384, a real annual return of 7.99 percent. Simply adding 10 percent more small-cap stocks improves returns without significantly increasing risks.

FIGURE 11–3 PREFERRED PORTFOLIO ALLOCATION

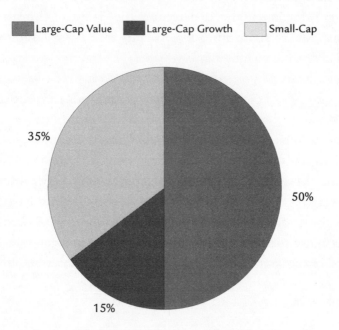

So, you might ask, why don't we increase the small-cap allocation even further? Rather surprisingly, if you increase the small-cap allocation to 45 percent, you actually *reduce* the performance while *increasing* risk! That's because of the underlying volatility of small-cap stocks; a 35 percent allocation manages to wrest the greatest possible value from core small-cap holdings.

Flexibility Is Key

You can easily implement both the conservative and preferred portfolio allocations in your 401(k), IRA, or brokerage account by using ETFs and mutual funds. For the conservative allocation, you would invest 25 percent of your portfolio in the iShares Russell 2000 Index, 60 percent in the iShares Russell 1000 Value Index, and 15 percent in the Vanguard Growth Viper Fund. For the preferred portfolio allocation, you would invest 35 percent in the iShares Russell 2000 Index, 50 percent in the iShares Russell 1000 Value Index, and 15 percent in the Vanguard Growth Viper Fund. Make sure to annually rebalance each portfolio to the target allocations, which allows you to harvest money from the strategy that has performed the best and direct it to the strategy that has done the worst. While this may sound counterintuitive, this allows you to funnel some money away from the hottest style and into the one that is just heating up. These two simple portfolios are a great way to maintain broad exposure to all of the investment styles and capitalization categories while periodically harvesting the best performers. If your 401(k) does not have ETFs, use the guidelines from chapter 9 to select the mutual funds with characteristics most closely aligned with each category.

Using Stock Selection Strategies to Allocate Your Portfolio

Now let's look at using the stock selection strategies featured in chapter 8 to build a portfolio that takes advantage of the trends I believe will emerge over the next twenty years. Here, we will allocate a bit more to the large-cap growth category, since we can use a growth strategy that includes value parameters. Thus, we will do a single allocation that should serve as a good core domestic equity holding over the next twenty years. We'll use all of the style-specific strategies featured in chapter 8 to build a portfolio with exposure to micro-cap and small-cap stocks, as well as to large-cap value and growth names that also include a value carburetor. Here's the allocation:

1. 10 percent in Tiny Titan micro-cap stocks;

2. 15 percent in the Cheap Stocks on the Mend Small-Cap Growth strategy;

3. 25 percent in the Dogs of the Dow;

4. 25 percent in the Market Leaders low Price-to-Cash Flow strategy;

5. 25 percent in the Market Leaders Growth strategy.

Figure 11–4 shows the allocation that we will maintain over the next twenty years. Thus, we maintain a mix of 75 percent large-cap stocks and 25 percent small- and micro-cap stocks by annually rebalancing the portfolio to maintain that mix. Here we can afford to allocate 25 percent of the portfolio to large-cap growth stocks since we can employ a more finely tuned strategy than the Vanguard Viper Growth Fund uses. This larger alloca-

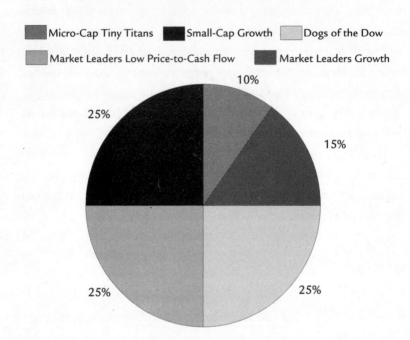

FIGURE 11–4 CUSTOM ALLOCATION
USING STOCK SELECTION STRATEGIES

tion gives us a greater chance of benefiting from those periods when large-cap growth stocks are performing well.

Historical Performance and Twenty-Year Rolling Returns

Historically, this customized portfolio allocation has dramatically outperformed a 75 percent S&P 500 allocation and a 25 percent small-cap allocation. Between December 31, 1952, and December 31, 2004, this portfolio mix had a real annual return of 14.46 percent, turning one dollar invested in 1952 into $1,121 by the end of 2004. By comparison, a 75 percent S&P 500 and 25 percent small-cap stock portfolio grew at a real rate of 8.32 percent over the same period, turning one dollar invested in 1952 into $64 at the end of 2004. The two strategies had similar risk, with the custom allocation sporting a standard deviation of return of 20.65 percent, versus 18.59 percent for the S&P 500/Small Stock allocation.

For all rolling twenty-year periods between 1972 and 2004, the worst this custom strategy ever performed was a real annual return of 8.95 percent and the best was a real annual return of 18.92 percent. The average for all rolling twenty-year periods was a real annual return of 13.15 percent. Over the same period, the worst the S&P 500/Small Stock portfolio ever performed was a real annual return of 3.01 percent; the best was 12.93 percent and the average for all rolling twenty-year periods between 1972 and 2004 was 7.05 percent.

Forecast for the Next Twenty Years

For all rolling twenty-year period average returns, our custom allocation did 6.10 percent better than the S&P 500/Small Stock combination. The forecasted return over the next twenty years for a portfolio 75 percent invested in the S&P 500 and 25 percent invested in small stocks would be a return between 4.15 percent and 6.15 percent. Thus, I forecast that for this custom strategy, real returns over the next twenty years should be between 10.25 and 12.25 percent. (I arrive at this estimate by adding the average 6.1 percent twenty-year excess return of the strategy to the minimum and maximum expected return of the S&P 500/Small Stock combination.)

Rather than adding that 6.1 percent premium to the S&P 500/Small Stock portfolio, let's try to be a bit more exacting and build this custom portfolio from the ground up, using the forecasts for each of the substrategies. By doing this the minimum forecasted return would be 9.54 percent and the maximum 11.54 percent.

We'll use these slightly lower forecasts to look at the growth of $100,000. If we achieved a return consistent with the low forecast, $100,000 would grow to $618,664 in twenty years, whereas if we achieved returns consistent with the high forecast, $100,000 would grow to $888,409. This is *significantly* higher than the returns we can achieve using the simpler conservative and preferred portfolios that utilize the Russell indexes and the Vanguard Viper Growth Fund, and reinforces the value of using stock selection strategies whenever possible. The significantly stronger performance of this custom portfolio could serve as a catalyst to hiring an advisor or setting up an IRA at an online broker specializing in basket trades so you can do it yourself.

Let's take a closer look at the custom portfolio. It currently holds eighty different stocks with a median market capitalization of $1 billion and has an average market capitalization of $20.5 billion. This large disparity between median and average market capitalization is due to the fact that the portfolio holds fifty tiny stocks, but the thirty big stocks still dominate the portfolio. Thus, even though 75 percent of your money is invested in large-cap stocks like Ford, GM, Merck, Intel, and Hewlett-Packard, the overall portfolio looks much different because of the inclusion of the much smaller stocks.

If you review the list of stocks meeting the portfolio's criteria at any given time, you'll likely see that there are many stocks you've never heard of, and those you are familiar with are probably out of favor on the street. While the obscurity and relative unpopularity of the stocks in this portfolio may give you pause, keep in mind that one of the key reasons this strategy works so well is precisely *because* it selects these types of stocks. Popular stocks are the easy bets that appeal to most investors. Remembering what we learned in chapter 6, it's in our very nature to prefer a stock that has the approval of other investors and the financial media. Those stocks tend to be overpriced and overhyped, typically sporting dangerously high PE ratios. You pay an enormous price for popularity and a cheery consensus, which could be seriously detrimental to your portfolio's health in a low return market environment.

The Benefits of Rebalancing and Annual Contributions

Let's look at the importance of annually rebalancing your portfolio. Table 11-1 shows the performance of the custom stock selection strategy portfolio over the *past* twenty years. Since we are looking at the returns for the strategies during the recent bull market, note that the portfolio's total return is much higher than we expect to see in the *next* twenty years. Each year the portfolio was rebalanced to the target allocations. You can see that even with lump-sum investing, rebalancing is vital; it has you remove money from the strategies that have been the most successful in the previous year and allocate it to those that have been the least successful. Look at the end of 2000: the micro-cap Tiny Titan strategy lost an atrocious 40 percent, whereas the Dogs of the Dow had a relatively strong year, gaining 2.91 percent during a bear market. Most investors would look at the great Dogs return and put *more* money into it, relegating the Tiny Titans to the wayside. Rebalancing forces you to do the opposite, taking money *away* from the Dogs and bringing the Tiny Titans allocation back up to 10 percent. In 2001 this move was richly rewarded, with the Tiny Titans up an impressive 58.7 percent compared to a loss of 6.35 percent for the Dogs of the Dow.

We've been looking at the results of making a lump-sum investment and then letting the market compound your portfolio over time. You can enhance your returns further by making ongoing contributions to your portfolio. Assume the example above was a 401(k) plan and you were able to make annual $15,000 con-

TABLE 11-1 RETURNS FOR CUSTOM ALLOCATION

Annual Returns						$100,000.00
			ML			Tiny Titan
	Tiny	Dogs	Growth	ML PCF	Small-Cap	Micro-Cap
	Titans	the Dow	10	10 REAL	Growth	REAL
						$10,000.00
Dec-86	5.43	26.69	15.42	0.71	7.65	$10,543.00
Dec-87	8.63	2.38	26.88	1.84	-11.13	$12,209.52
Dec-88	6.67	16.84	10.69	25.26	18.88	$12,824.70
Dec-89	22.24	21.71	69.53	11.04	20.66	$17,150.47
Dec-90	-16.25	-13.2	-6.2	-26.69	-4.34	$15,380.27
Dec-91	66.96	34.87	44.67	55.91	51.51	$26,430.56
Dec-92	19.35	12.15	6.6	10.02	52.09	$28,016.48
Dec-93	38.59	24.77	8.29	35.64	17.82	$38,044.32
Dec-94	-29.67	1.29	0.91	3.47	-15.28	$23,883.22
Dec-95	66.99	34.29	18.99	19.03	12.88	$54,529.35
Dec-96	20.17	24.46	26.35	18.35	19.91	$49,721.21
Dec-97	46.02	20.15	49.79	31.02	17.14	$73,885.86
Dec-98	-3.23	8.94	52.07	22.79	15.3	$64,826.62
Dec-99	-14.6	1.28	78.07	82	61.3	$70,334.29
Dec-00	-40.03	2.91	-25.66	-11.82	-5.32	$73,133.73
Dec-01	58.7	-6.35	-7.3	16.95	6.2	$167,517.54
Dec-02	12.9	-11.02	-14.98	-7.83	-3.98	$128,259.77
Dec-03	141.19	26.33	29.2	87.7	54.26	$252,728.32
Dec-04	21.35	1.11	12.4	12.28	32.39	$200,988.63

WITH LUMP SUM INVESTMENT OF $100,000

Starting Capital Dogs of the Dow REAL	ML Growth 10 REAL	ML Low PCFL 10 REAL	Small-Cap Growth REAL	Portfolio
$25,000.00	$25,000.00	$25,000.00	$15,000.00	
$31,672.50	$28,855.00	$25,177.50	$16,147.50	$112,395.50
$28,767.63	$35,651.85	$28,615.89	$14,982.88	$120,227.78
$35,118.53	$33,270.03	$37,649.33	$21,439.02	$140,301.61
$42,690.27	$59,463.33	$38,947.73	$25,393.19	$183,644.99
$39,850.96	$43,064.75	$33,657.54	$26,351.22	$158,304.73
$53,376.40	$57,254.87	$61,703.23	$35,977.13	$234,742.18
$65,815.84	$62,558.79	$64,565.84	$53,552.91	$274,509.85
$85,626.48	$74,316.68	$93,086.29	$48,514.13	$339,587.90
$85,992.15	$85,669.54	$87,842.90	$43,154.83	$326,542.63
$109,628.52	$97,138.27	$97,170.92	$55,290.20	$413,757.27
$128,740.57	$130,695.58	$122,420.43	$74,420.45	$505,998.24
$151,989.22	$189,483.69	$165,739.72	$88,908.95	$670,007.45
$182,476.53	$254,720.08	$205,675.54	$115,877.79	$823,586.56
$208,532.12	$366,640.15	$374,731.89	$199,266.77	$1,219,505.21
$313,748.20	$226,645.04	$268,839.92	$173,194.13	$1,055,561.03
$247,133.23	$244,626.27	$308,619.66	$168,150.87	$1,136,047.56
$252,713.78	$241,466.91	$261,773.76	$163,624.93	$1,047,839.15
$330,933.80	$338,452.04	$491,698.52	$242,459.50	$1,656,272.18
$418,664.20	$465,412.48	$464,915.60	$328,910.81	**$1,878,891.73**

TABLE 11-2 RETURNS

Annual Returns						$100,000.00
			ML			Tiny Titan
	Tiny	Dogs	Growth	ML PCF	Small-Cap	Micro-Cap
	Titans	the Dow	10	10 REAL	Growth	REAL
						$10,000.00
Dec-86	5.43	26.69	15.42	0.71	7.65	$10,543.00
Dec-87	8.63	2.38	26.88	1.84	-11.13	$13,838.97
Dec-88	6.67	16.84	10.69	25.26	18.88	$16,136.30
Dec-89	22.24	21.71	69.53	11.04	20.66	$23,412.67
Dec-90	-16.25	-13.2	-6.2	-26.69	-4.34	$22,252.36
Dec-91	66.96	34.87	44.67	55.91	51.51	$40,744.46
Dec-92	19.35	12.15	6.6	10.02	52.09	$44,979.51
Dec-93	38.59	24.77	8.29	35.64	17.82	$63,157.72
Dec-94	-29.67	1.29	0.91	3.47	-15.28	$40,703.69
Dec-95	66.99	34.29	18.99	19.03	12.88	$95,438.15
Dec-96	20.17	24.46	26.35	18.35	19.91	$88,825.41
Dec-97	46.02	20.15	49.79	31.02	17.14	$134,185.12
Dec-98	-3.23	8.94	52.07	22.79	15.3	$119,202.22
Dec-99	-14.6	1.28	78.07	82	61.3	$130,590.69
Dec-00	-40.03	2.91	-25.66	-11.82	-5.32	$136,687.99
Dec-01	58.7	-6.35	-7.3	16.95	6.2	$315,473.19
Dec-02	12.9	-11.02	-14.98	-7.83	-3.98	$243,235.49
Dec-03	141.19	26.33	29.2	87.7	54.26	$482,899.06
Dec-04	21.35	1.11	12.4	12.28	32.39	$385,858.02

WITH ANNUAL $15,000 CONTRIBUTION INCLUDED

Starting Capital Dogs of the Dow REAL	ML Growth 10 REAL	ML Low PCFL 10 REAL	Small-Cap Growth REAL	Portfolio
$25,000.00	$25,000.00	$25,000.00	$15,000.00	
$31,672.50	$28,855.00	$25,177.50	$16,147.50	$127,395.50
$32,606.88	$40,409.85	$32,434.89	$16,982.46	$151,273.06
$44,186.86	$41,861.04	$47,371.16	$26,975.01	$191,530.36
$58,277.90	$81,175.36	$53,168.83	$34,665.08	$265,699.84
$57,656.86	$62,306.61	$48,696.14	$38,125.27	$244,037.24
$82,283.26	$88,262.17	$95,119.62	$55,461.12	$376,870.63
$105,665.10	$100,436.02	$103,658.27	$85,977.38	$455,716.28
$142,149.30	$123,373.79	$154,533.39	$80,538.74	$578,752.94
$146,554.71	$146,004.90	$149,708.92	$73,547.92	$571,520.14
$191,873.60	$170,012.95	$170,070.11	$96,769.79	$739,164.60
$229,991.07	$233,483.62	$218,700.33	$132,949.84	$918,950.26
$276,029.69	$344,123.90	$301,002.16	$161,468.75	$1,231,809.61
$335,483.35	$468,303.22	$378,134.76	$213,041.47	$1,529,165.01
$387,184.58	$680,746.03	$695,770.08	$369,981.47	$2,279,272.86
$586,399.92	$423,602.86	$502,465.70	$323,702.33	$1,987,858.81
$465,407.44	$460,686.28	$581,200.22	$316,665.91	$2,154,433.05
$479,253.63	$457,924.74	$496,435.23	$310,302.99	$2,002,152.09
$632,329.68	$646,695.13	$939,509.87	$463,277.97	$3,179,711.72
$803,751.63	$893,498.99	$892,545.08	$631,443.05	**$3,622,096.77**

tributions for the next twenty years. Look at the difference in your portfolio's final value in table 11–2. Instead of the $1,878,892 you'd have at the end of 2004 with a $100,000 lump sum investment made twenty years earlier, you would have a portfolio valued at $3,622,097! All from making annual $15,000 contributions for nineteen years! This additional $285,000 in contributions would add $1,458,205 to your portfolio's final value. Clearly, this is one of the best things you can do to ensure that you maximize your portfolio's potential, particularly in a low return environment.

What About Bonds?

For investors looking to maximize their returns over the next twenty years, bonds are currently a poor choice. Remember that the inflation-adjusted twenty-year Treasury is currently yielding only 1.70 percent, hardly a rate that will build a healthy retirement portfolio. That doesn't mean that bonds can't have a place in your portfolio, particularly if you're nearing retirement or wish to reduce your portfolio's volatility. It simply means that the returns you will earn for this reduction of volatility will be quite low if you invest in them now. My advice is to begin your investment with a 100 percent allocation to equities and watch bond yields. When the yield on the TIPS surpasses the forecasted growth rates for the various equity classes covered in this book, begin to shift a portion of your portfolio into bonds.

For example, if the yield on the inflation-protected Treasury goes above 4 percent, consider reducing your equity allocation by 15 percent, the amount we currently have allocated to large-cap growth stocks. Keep in mind that you would not stop investing in that category, but rather reducing the equity allocation of your portfolio by 15 percent and investing that percentage in bonds. Thus, if you have $200,000 in your portfolio when the yield exceeds 4 percent, you would move from a 100 percent equity allocation to 85 percent equities and 15 percent bonds, with $170,000 invested in equities and $30,000 in bonds. As the bond yield increases, you might continue to increase your portfolio's fixed income allocation.

Should bond yields get very high again—a distinct possibility given the underlying demographic trends and the government's needs to finance the retirements of 78 million baby boomers—it would be prudent to increase your bond allocation. For example, if bond yields went higher than our forecast for large-cap value stocks, you would shift to an allocation that was mostly fixed income.

Other Allocations

In this chapter, my intention was to give you basic core equity allocation advice. For most investors, equities make up the bulk of their portfolio. I hope my allocation advice is flexible enough so as not to matter what type of investment account you have. Obviously, there are many additional asset classes and styles you can consider as the next twenty years unfold. The most important (that are beyond the scope of this book) are international equities and bonds, domestic alternative investments such as long-short hedge funds, private equity and venture capital, emerging market equities, and commodities. If you work with a good investment advisor, he or she should discuss these with you. They might also show you add-on strategies such as writing covered call options to increase the income in your portfolio. All of these can make sense depending upon your age and how much time you have left until you need to begin consuming your portfolio's capital.

I've also left domestic real estate out of the investment mix, as many of us already own a home and for the most part should be using it as shelter rather than for speculation. As I mentioned in chapter 2, the huge spurt in housing prices that we have seen over the last six years is unlikely to continue. Housing's long-term real rate of return in the United States has been just slightly better than an investment in U.S. T-bills. That's because housing prices have remained closely aligned with incomes, with the percentage of income allocated to housing remaining remarkably stable over time. The increase in U.S. home prices over the last six years is due to low interest rates and innovative mortgage structures that allow for interest-only adjustable rate mortgages. Because rates are so low, a home buyer with an average income is able to buy considerably more house than in the past. When rates shift, however, that trend will end. Many of the people who stretched to meet payments under the lower rates will be unable to continue making those payments, which will lead to a housing glut. Increased supply will drive prices down, ending the speculative trend. At the time of this writing, single family homes are near the top of their return cycle and are unlikely to continue their upward ascent. Historically, real estate is a distant second to equities, and that relationship is likely to continue in the future.

Big Differences from Asset Allocation

In this chapter, I hope I've demonstrated how important it is to carefully allocate your portfolio as we move into the low return environment of the next twenty years. Simply by shifting from the currently popular mix of core large-cap strategies like the S&P 500 and large-cap growth stocks you can *materially* improve the value of your portfolio twenty years from now. By just moving to the preferred portfolio that invests 35 percent in small-cap stocks and 65 percent in large-cap stocks with a value bias, you can potentially increase the value of your portfolio from $182,373 to

$320,215, and this is if we only achieve the minimum of my forecasts for the next twenty years. If you're willing to do the little extra work that using our stock selection strategies entails, you could push this to $618,664 at the end of twenty years (still assuming the minimum forecasted returns). That's a huge advantage and only requires a few hours of work each year to rebalance your portfolio. I doubt you could find any job that pays you so well on an hourly basis! The point is clear—over the next twenty years, allocation will be extremely important to your financial well-being.

Chapter Eleven Highlights

◆ How you allocate your portfolio will profoundly affect your portfolio's performance over the next twenty years. If you maintain the traditional 50 percent large-cap core, 40 percent large-cap value, and 10 percent small-cap allocation currently adhered to by millions of Americans, your total real rate of return over the next twenty years will probably fall between 3.05 and 5.05 percent per year.

◆ The conservative allocation maintains a portfolio mix similar to the overall market: 75 percent in large-cap stocks and 25 percent in small and mid-size companies. To take advantage of the coming twenty-year trends, you should have more large-cap value than large-cap growth stocks. All of my recommended allocations include a large-cap growth component to take advantage of those periods when large-cap growth stocks are in favor.

◆ The preferred allocation increases the small-cap stock allocation to 35 percent. Increasing it further has little effect on total return but increases the portfolio's volatility. You can use both the conservative and preferred portfolio allocations in your 401(k), IRA, and traditional brokerage account using ETFs and mutual funds.

◆ By using specific time-tested stock selection strategies, you can dramatically improve your portfolio's expected real rate of return. The recommended allocation increases the investment in large-cap growth stocks, since you are able to include a value parameter that reduces the likelihood of buying overvalued stocks. You will need a brokerage account or an advisor account to implement these strategies.

◆ Investors seeking the highest total return should begin with a 100 percent equity allocation. As bond yields increase, move money from equities to bonds. Thus, if bond yields exceed our long-term forecast for large-cap growth stocks, move 15 percent of your portfolio to bonds and maintain the balance in equities. If yields continue to rise above other equity forecasts, move that percentage from stocks to bonds.

12

Putting It All Together

If you don't know where you're going, you'll end
up somewhere else.

—Yogi Berra

Thus far, I've covered what direction investment markets are most likely to take over the next twenty years and which
equity and bond allocations are likely to offer the highest returns.
Long-term reversion to the mean suggests that you should invest
the bulk of your assets in large-cap value, small-cap, and high-
dividend-yielding strategies. I've shown you how you can use these
trends to your advantage, and how you can use mutual funds, exchange traded funds, and stock selection strategies to help you
make these allocations.

Knowing and doing are two very different things, however. I
have been a professional money manager for more than fifteen
years, and if experience has taught me anything, it is that you

must have the will to implement investment strategies in a consistent and diligent manner. Sure, it *sounds* simple, but things get very messy in real time. In the here and now, a century of facts pales in comparison with the daily excitement of an out-of-control equity bubble or crushing bear market. In real time, we read business magazines and watch CNBC, getting caught up in any strategy that is working right now, with little thought about how well it might do over a very long period of time. Our very nature conspires to rob us of the ability to stay the course with our investment strategies.

Advisor Help Preferred

In a moment I will show you how to implement all of the strategies discussed here on your own, but first a word of caution. Unless you have the emotional makeup of *Star Trek*'s Mr. Spock, I am fairly certain that at some point in the process of trying to do this yourself, you will throw in the towel and not be able to stick with the program. Why? Because of the very essence of our human nature. As we saw in chapter 6, knowing about our foibles does not make them go away.

Research from the new field of neuroeconomics suggests that the wiring of our nervous systems frequently prevents us from making sensible long-term investment decisions. According to the Center for the Study of Neuroeconomics at George Mason University, "Neuroeconomics is the study of how the embodied brain interacts with its external environment to produce economic behavior. Research in this field will allow social scientists to better understand individual decision making and consequently to better predict economic behavior." Early research indicates that even when we logically understand what we should do, our brain processes our choices through its emotional centers, negating the power of factual choice. The result is that many people reject underlying logic and empirical facts in favor of an emotional response.

In my many years of experience, I have seen this happen time and again. I had several clients at my former firm, O'Shaughnessy Capital Management, who decided that they could save themselves the investment management fees by investing their portfolios on their own. They reasoned—quite rightly I should add—that they had access to the various formulas and selection strategies in *What Works on Wall Street* and that they could easily do it on their own. What they didn't count on was how much their emotions would get in the way. Of all the people who fired us to go it on their own, the vast majority wound up rehiring us! They discovered that they could not invest dispassionately, as their own prejudices about various stocks overwhelmed their logical facilities. Thus, if you really want to *achieve* results like I believe are possible, I think you are best served with the help of a dispassionate, professional advisor. For now, in the interest of thoroughness, let's see how you can do this on your own.

Online Research and Brokers

For those of you who want to use the stock selection strategies featured in chapter 8, the easiest place to start is at MSN.com at www.moneycentral.msn.com/investor/home.asp, where you'll find a free—yet nevertheless robust—stock screening utility. By downloading the Deluxe Stock Screener, you can run the screens discussed in chapter 8. For example, one of the predefined screens at MSN brings you the current Dogs of the Dow stocks. Simply go to the predefined screen menu and select Dogs of the Dow. As of this writing, GM is at the top and GE is at the bottom of the list, and the dividend yield of the ten-stock portfolio is 4.14 percent. You can export this list directly to Excel to check ticker symbols, dividend yield, and so on.

Using Criteria from *The Markets of Tomorrow* or *What Works on Wall Street*

You can also run any of the other models I've highlighted as having great potential over the coming twenty years. For example, the micro-cap growth and value strategy that buys stocks with market capitalizations between $25 million and $250 million, price-to-sales ratios equal to or less than one, and then buys the twenty-five stocks with the best twelve-month price appreciation is a snap at the MSN site. Simply select the *Deluxe Screener,* start a new screen and under *company basics,* choose "market capitalization" and set it between $25 million and $250 million. Then move on to *price ratios* and select "price/sales ratio" and set it to equal to or less than one. Finally, under *stock price history* select "% Price change last year" and select high as possible. Making sure that you've set your selected returns to twenty-five matches, run the screen. The twenty-five stocks that currently meet the screen's criteria will appear. After exporting the list to Excel, we see that the current twenty-five stocks have an average market capitalization of $93.7 million, an average price-to-sales ratio of 0.56, and have, on average, gained 235 percent over the previous twelve months.

More Power for a Price

If you want more screening capabilities and the ability to segment a database by factor deciles and can't afford the considerable institutional price of COMPUSTAT, I recommend the Value Line

Investment Survey software available at www.valueline.com. The Value Line Investment Analyzer costs $598 per year and offers access to eight thousand stocks with over three hundred data fields to generate screens similar to those featured in chapter 8.

With this software, it's a snap to generate deciles, and all of the screens run in an intuitive manner. This might be more horsepower than many investors need, but the database covers virtually every stock available and offers you access to Value Line's famous Timeliness and Safety rankings, which can be very useful if you get hooked on stock screening strategies. You can also use this database to create our Market Leaders universe that we use in several of the stock selection strategies featured in chapter 8.

Online Specialty Brokerages

If you want to invest on your own in strategies like those featured here, you'll want to open an account at one of the online brokers that specialize in basket trades. Two of the best are Foliofn (www.foliofn.com) and ShareBuilder (www.sharebuilder.com). Both allow you to invest in baskets of stocks for one low annual subscription fee. Thus, the number of individual stocks you buy won't matter, as trades are covered in the subscription fees. You can also use these online brokerage accounts to purchase ETFs and mutual funds to round out your overall portfolio.

At Foliofn, a basic Bronze membership costs $19.95 per month or $199 per year. It allows for two hundred free window trades per month, far more than what these annually rebalanced portfolios require. Keep in mind that for accounts of under $100,000 your annual fee will be a higher percentage of your assets than if you invested in the ETFs featured in chapter 10. With an account of more than $100,000, you'll pay about 20 basis points in fees, roughly equal to that of most of the ETFs featured here. As a percentage of assets, the more money you have in your account, the lower your fees.

Where's the Catch?

On the face of it, *everyone* should be managing their money online using these simple yet effective methods at the lowest cost available. So why does *anyone* work with an advisor anymore? The simple answer is discipline, follow-through, and perseverance. Sadly, most of us lack all three. While it's easy to *say* that you will be disciplined, my experience has taught me that at the first sign of market volatility, most investors begin second-guessing their strategy. The very ease of use these online brokerages offer also leads to a big problem for investors—they tend to look at their portfolio's performance *far too often*. A few months can seem like an eternity when your strategy is out of favor. I used to tell prospective clients that if they wanted access to all of my strategies, all they had to do was buy a copy of *What Works on Wall Street*. But if they actually wanted the strategies to work, the annual investment management fee charged by my firm was money well spent.

Take the micro-cap strategy from chapter 8 I just discussed. What if you had read about the strategy in June of 1998 and decided to go it alone? You fund an online brokerage account, run the list of names and buy them. Then you start to watch, and you start to worry. In June, the portfolio lost a real 3.71 percent, whereas the broader indexes of large-cap stocks like the S&P 500 actually *grew* a real 3.93 percent. Just one month in the game and you're already wondering how you got yourself in such a pickle. Yet you manage to stick it out, reasoning that the strategy had such great long-term results.

Your portfolio does even worse in July, losing a real 7.37 percent in value. Yikes! How could I have been so stupid? Damn that O'Shaughnessy for ever talking about this crazy strategy, for while it might have worked in the past, it doesn't work anymore. The emotional part of your brain would most likely have taken over at this point—and it wouldn't be focusing on long-term statistics. Rather, it would be thinking about *your* portfolio and how horribly it has performed. You'd deeply regret pursuing something so "risky," and you would be ashamed to have been suckered into it.

Then comes August, and the coup de grâce—your portfolio drops a stunning 21.10 percent as the woes of Asia and Russia hit small-cap stocks with a vengeance. One of the largest hedge funds in the country, Long-Term Capital Management, has melted down and small-cap stocks everywhere are reeling, but none of this will matter to you. From the moment you bought your stocks they have lost money, and you would now be looking at a three-month loss of over 30 percent. If you started with $100,000, three months after investing in the strategy you'd have only $70,000 left. It wouldn't matter to you in the least that other small-cap stocks got trounced as well. Those three hellish months would leave you emotionally battered and lacking any confidence in the strategy, and you would undoubtedly have some pretty choice things to say to me if given the chance. If you were like the vast majority of investors at that time, you would have thrown in the towel after just three months, swearing you would never take such risks again.

Why Advice Is Worth It

Nick Murray—the dean of the art of selling financial advice—calls do-it-yourself investing "no-help" investing because you have no one to rely on when the going gets rough. All of the available research shows us that for perfectly rational investors, doing it yourself costs the least and makes the most sense. Once human behavior is factored in, however, you are *much better off* working with an advisor. Remember the Dalbar study featured earlier in the book? The actual returns earned by rapid-fire do-it-yourself investors paled in comparison with those of investors who worked with an advisor. Since the only goal is to earn the highest returns, what makes the most sense is to take the path that will give you the best chance of getting there. All of the empirical evidence suggests that investors who work with a financial advisor earn the best long-term returns, so let's look at how to find the right advisor.

What to Look for in a Broker or Financial Advisor

Think of your advisor the way you think of your doctor—you might read a lot about how to cure a health problem that you have, you may bring in articles and discuss them with your doctor, but in the end you're going to rely on your doctor for his or her prognosis and recommended therapy. The same should hold true with your broker or advisor. The best financial advisors or brokers will work with you on a fee-only basis, generally charging a certain percentage of assets under management for an entire investment program. As this is a very important relationship, ask hard questions. Ask to speak with other clients. Ask to see how he or she has implemented other investment programs. Make sure they have executed the plans in a disciplined and dispassionate manner. Ask to see allocations that they have recommended to others with circumstances similar to your own.

The most important thing to look for is intellectual honesty and a real track record of discipline and consistency. An advisor who invested heavily in large-cap growth at the end of the 1990s at the expense of small-cap and large-cap value stocks should get a red flag. Avoid them. They have shown you that they are just as naïve and gullible as an investor going it alone.

You should look for an advisor or broker with a history of managing money with a straightforward and carefully considered asset allocation. Demand to see that they stuck with their allocations through thick and thin. This discipline is vital to successful portfolio management.

Some of the best brokers and advisors I have worked with also have a keen understanding of the human psyche and how it trips us up at exactly the wrong time. They are excellent listeners and mindful of their clients' psychological state, standing ready to reel them in when emotions take over. In this sense, they are the ideal wingman for their clients, getting them back on course when the market gets turbulent.

Finally, don't hire anyone who starts off with stories about what a great stock picker he is or how he managed to perfectly time the market. An advisor who does this is not likely to stick with long-term allocations. They will be guilty of all the sins you could just as easily commit on your own—chasing performance and reacting emotionally chief among them. Discipline, a long-term outlook, and a dispassionate interest in helping you reach your goals as an investor are the hallmarks of a good advisor, so demand them. That is what you are paying them for.

Outsource Your Anxiety

Unless you're a real stock market junkie, wouldn't you rather outsource your anxiety to someone else? After finding an advisor or broker who meets all of the important criteria, hold them responsible. The best advisors and brokers I've worked with often outline what they will do for a client and make the client sign an agreement. That way, when the advisor is doing the tough job of keeping you committed to an underperforming asset class despite your objections, he or she will be able to show you in writing that this is the very thing you hired them for in the first place.

If you agree with the data in this book, give a copy to your advisor and ask them what they think. The best advisors will give you an honest answer. If they find this research compelling they will help you allocate your portfolio to take advantage of the trends. Since this book only covers investing in long equities and bonds, a good advisor should also be able to offer ways to enhance your portfolio even more. For example, I think investors with the appropriate means should seriously consider investing in long-short hedge funds, as they have low correlations with equities and bonds and should do extremely well in low-return environments.

Another asset class worth discussing with an advisor is commodities. Because they are beyond the scope of this book, I won't go into detail here, but they are worth considering because they also have low correlations with stocks and bonds and thus can be a good hedge in a diversified portfolio. A good advisor will help you add these to your portfolio, when appropriate.

If your advisor is using a mix of separate accounts, ETFs, and mutual funds, expect them to rebalance your portfolio in a timely manner. It's their job to stay on top of any portfolio managers you've hired, making sure the manager is sticking with the style they were hired to implement. It's also their job to make sure that your portfolio stays on track with your grand plan. They should meet with you annually to review your performance and find out whether anything material has changed in your life. They should reinforce why you are doing what you're doing and alert you to any changes that have been made or are worth consideration.

It is also their job to keep you from reacting emotionally to your portfolio's performance over the short term. If you find yourself in emotional discussions with your broker or advisor, remind yourself that it is their job to talk you down off the ledge! Outsource your anxiety and let *them* worry. Chances are, you'll wind up with better long-term results and fewer gray hairs.

Meanwhile, Back to Those Micro-Caps

Let's return to the story of the micro-cap strategy and its sorry performance in the summer of 1998. Rather than going it alone, what if you had hired a good advisor who refused to let you throw in the towel, reminding you of the reason you chose the strategy in the first place? Even after your initial $30,000 loss in that horrific summer of 1998, by the end of December of 2004, the $100,000 would be worth $188,000, a real annual return of 11.97 percent. The same $100,000 invested in the S&P 500—which seemed to be the best investment back in 1998—would have returned a paltry 0.71 percent over the same period, with the $100,000 growing to just $104,782. A good advisor would have been worth twice their fee if they helped you make just that *one* crucial choice in those seemingly desperate days of 1998. Like the old joke about an anesthesiologist's job being hours and hours of boredom punctuated by minutes of sheer terror, the best advisors earn the bulk of their fees with a few portfolio-saving plays.

Chapter Twelve Highlights

◆ All of the tools you need to implement the strategies and advice offered in this book are readily available. To use ETFs, all you need is a 401(k), an IRA, or a traditional brokerage account. For stock selection strategies, you can use MSN Investor or the Value Line database. If you invest on your own, always remember what an emotional roller coaster it can be and how difficult it can be to adhere to even the most carefully crafted plans.

◆ Investors are far more likely to achieve their goals if they work with a financial advisor. Research conducted by Dalbar Associates indicates that investors working with brokers or advisors enjoy higher rates of returns than those who do it on their own.

◆ When looking for an advisor, seek one who relies on asset allocation rather than their ability as a market timer or stock picker. Ask to review their track record and advice they have given in the past. Ask their opinion of my recommendations in this book. Good advisors will tell you what they like and what they don't, and will back up their opinions with facts rather than opinions.

◆ Good advisors will also help round out the core domestic equity and bond advice offered here. They will show you the benefits of adding asset classes and employing alternative investment strategies and will explain how what they advocate might affect your expected returns.

13

The Fast Approaching Future: The Markets of Tomorrow Will Soon Be the Markets of Today

> The further backward you look, the further forward you can see.
>
> —Winston Churchill

Many people will view my attempt to forecast the market over the next twenty years as the height of hubris. After all, most forecasters have *dismal* shorter-term track records, so why put any faith into what I have to say about the next two decades? If no one can get *this year* right, how can I expect to know what might transpire over the next twenty years?

When it comes to predicting the market, I believe most forecasters have their priorities exactly backward. Warren Buffett has said that "in the short run the stock market is a voting machine, but in the long run it's a weighing machine." That is exactly why most prognosticators get their forecasts wrong—in the short term, there is too much noise caused by that short-term voting. When you graph real market returns on a rolling twelve-month basis, the results look chaotic: figure 13–1 would scare all but the most risk-seeking investors out of the market. Had you been unlucky enough to invest your money in the market in June of 1931, twelve months later you would have lost an astounding 64 percent of your portfolio! More recently, look at the results of putting your nest egg in the market on September 30, 2000—one year later, you'd have lost nearly 30 percent. Conversely, had you been gutsy enough to invest in the market near the horrifying lows of June 1932, twelve months later your account would have swelled by more than 182 percent!

When focusing on the short term, all we see is meaningless, frightening, and mostly trendless volatility. That's the historical backdrop for all of our fearless short-term forecasters. It's no surprise that we usually get the short term wrong, since it exhibits the greatest volatility. The ups and downs of the market are crazier still when you shorten your time frame to three months, a typical review period for portfolio managers. Figure 13–2 shows the total real three-month returns for the S&P 500 between 1927 and 2004. There is no signal here, only noise.

The noise quiets down considerably when we extend our time frame. Figure 13–3 shows the rolling real returns for all five-year periods. The story the data tells now becomes much clearer and a narrative begins to emerge that was absolutely lost on a review of the shorter-term numbers. When we extend our time frame even further, to ten-, fifteen-, and the twenty-year periods we've been using in this book, the data really begin to paint a much clearer picture of how the market moves from being undervalued to over-

FIGURE 13–1 REAL ROLLING 12-MONTH RETURN FOR S&P 500, 1927–2004

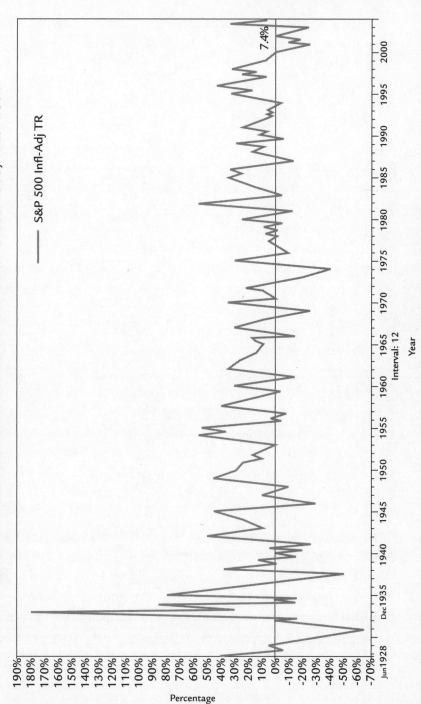

S&P 500 Infl-Adj TR

FIGURE 13–2 REAL ROLLING 3-MONTH RETURNS FOR S&P 500, 1927–2004

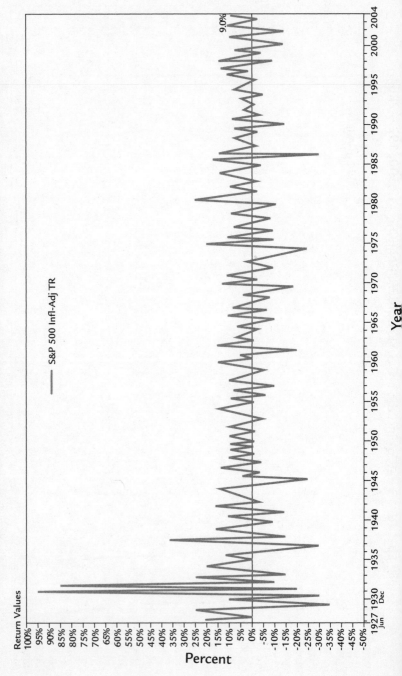

FIGURE 13-3 REAL ROLLING 5-YEAR RETURN FOR S&P 500, 1927–2004

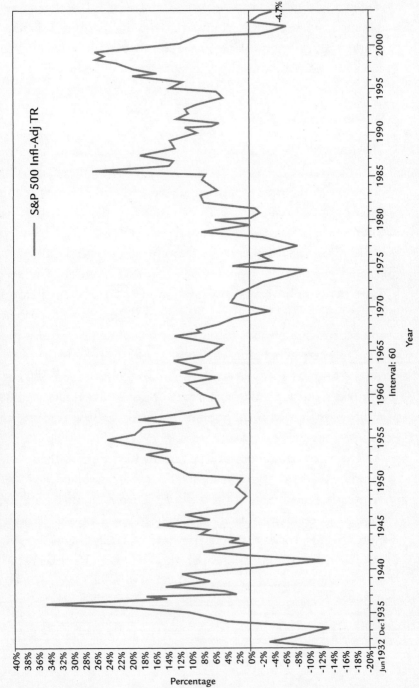

valued over time. By focusing on the long term, we see the market moving from a voting machine to a weighing machine. What appears to be scary and volatile in the short term winds up being an excellent choice for most investors over the long term.

So Close and Yet So Far

The year 1986 feels like yesterday—yet it also feels like a long time ago. Movies like *Top Gun* and *Ferris Bueller's Day Off* don't seem *that* old. Most of us remember where we were when we learned of the space shuttle *Challenger*'s fiery demise or of the news that the Chernobyl nuclear power plant had melted down.

And yet, 1986 also seems like another era altogether. IBM unveiled the first laptop computer, called the PC convertible. The Dow Jones Industrial Average hovered around 1,700. The Tax Reform Act of 1986 lowered the top tax rate from 50 percent to 28 percent and set the capital gains tax at the ordinary tax rate. Equity and bond markets were hardly the popular investments that they are today. For the twenty years ending January 1986, the S&P 500 had bumped along at a real rate of return of just 2.16 percent per year, and the long government bond had actually *lost* 0.39 percent per year over the previous twenty years.

The oldest baby boomers were turning forty in 1986, their peak spending years still several years off. The mutual fund industry was in its early adolescence—at the start of 1986, total mutual fund equity assets were approximately $117 billion spread across 579 equity mutual funds. Today, that figure is nearly $4.4 trillion spread across more than 4,500 funds! Simply put, although the bull market began in 1982, few investors expected it would last through March of 2000.

Brave New World

Whether it seems near or far, we've come a long way since 1986. Who could have predicted all that has happened in twenty years? In 1986 would you have believed me if I told you that the former Soviet Union would have collapsed and disappeared? That the former USSR satellite states including Poland, Estonia, Hungary, and the Czech Republic would be members of the European Union? Could you have imagined that Nelson Mandela, who was in a maximum security prison off the coast of Cape Town in 1986, would have been released and gone on to become the president of South Africa?

Of course, there are also the more frightening developments. Could anyone in 1986 imagine that terrorists would bring down the World Trade Center using our own planes as weapons? Or that the U.S. response would topple the regimes in Afghanistan and Iraq? Or that random bag checks on subways and planes and machine-gun-toting soldiers at major train stations and airports would become commonplace?

Could you have guessed at the mass proliferation of cell phones, wireless e-mail devices, and iPods? In 1986, when fax machines were still a novelty, could you even have imagined everyone with e-mail? Could you have imagined a movie like *The Matrix*? More important for investors, could *anyone* in 1986 have believed how ubiquitous the Internet and personal computers would be? eBay, Yahoo!, Amazon, and Google have a current combined market capitalization of nearly $172 billion and *none* of them were even *ideas* in 1986! Microsoft, with a current market capitalization of nearly $300 billion, was a privately owned software company issuing its first version of Windows. At its initial public offering in March of 1986, it had a market capitalization of $597 million. All of these events would have been virtually impossible to imagine twenty years ago, yet we take them for granted now and find nothing particularly extraordinary about them.

Investors of the mid-1980s had been trained by a lifetime of experience that stock rallies were quickly followed by declines. They knew from "personal experience" that if you wanted to make money, you invested in real estate, collectibles, or gold. If you were conservative, you simply kept your money in the bank earning interest. The majority of assets in 1986 still resided in banks and money market funds. Most investors simply couldn't conceive of what was to come—the greatest bull market and the greatest twenty-year returns for long-term government bonds in history.

If an investor in 1986 had access to the information contained in this book and the foresight to focus on decades instead of days, do you think he or she would have acted upon it? We've seen that people are much more comfortable reacting to or trying to predict short-term trends, yet in the market the short term is mostly noise. Our day-to-day lives usually blind us to longer-term trends. The million-dollar question we must now address is whether we will actually *use* this long-term data to assist us in our investment choices, for what it tells us about the next twenty years will be the key to our portfolio's health in the world of 2026.

The Likely Future

As all the political, social, and economic change that occurred between 1986 and 2006 has shown, it's virtually impossible to know what the world will look like in 2026. In all likelihood there will be a host of new companies and industries that simply don't exist today. Quantum computers may replace those we use now. Bioengineering may extend life expectancy to one hundred and beyond. Nanotechnology companies might replace Internet firms as the favorites of stock market speculators.

Along with many uncertainties, there are some trends in place now that can help us make some fairly good educated guesses about other things. The populations of all of the developed economies will be older—according to the Organization for Economic Development (OECD), by 2030 the number of people over age sixty-five across the developed world will have *increased* by 89 million, whereas the number of working-age adults will have *decreased* by 34 million. The number of workers supporting each retiree will also decline precipitously, from seven in 1960 to fewer than three by 2026.

If current trends continue, by 2026 India will be the third or fourth largest economy in the world, with China close on its heels. Indeed, China is forecasted to be the second largest economy in the world by the middle of the century. The power base of the economic world has already begun to shift, but by 2026 many of the now nascent trends will be obvious to even the most casual observers. News stories that would seem bizarre to us now will be commonplace in twenty years.

Human Nature Will Not Change

But there are likely to be many constants along the way as well. First and foremost is human nature. As we've seen from analyzing nearly two hundred years of data, the rolling twenty-year real rate of return to financial markets ebbs and flows with a remarkable degree of consistency, primarily because human beings are responsible for the economic and stock market cycles. While the *types* of companies and industries that get us excited has and will continue to change over time, our *reactions* to them will remain the same—we'll get unusually excited about the new and overprice it and be blasé about the old and underprice it.

Be it steamboats, railroads, telegraph and telephones, automobiles, motion pictures, radio, TV, aluminum, "space-age" technology, the first computer makers, Internet stocks, nanotechnology, or quantum computers, our *human* reactions to innovation are sure to persist. Just as in the past, we will more than likely drive their valuations to unsustainable levels. Our basic human nature is probably more responsible for the long-term ebbs and flows in the market than any single economic event or innovation. And since they are unlikely to change, we can infer that they will help us identify what will most likely happen over the next twenty years.

The Hard Facts

First, we must examine what the data tells us is the most likely future for stock and bond investors. Examining over two hundred years of financial data reveals that U.S. markets have a strong tendency to revert to the mean. In other words, in all of the rolling twenty-year periods we can study, the vast majority of twenty-year periods with strong performance were followed by periods offering meager returns. This can be explained from a valuation perspective, since we see that over the twenty-year periods that offered investors outstanding returns, there was a concurrent expansion of the market's PE ratio and a decline in the dividend yield paid out to investors.

The twenty-year ebb and flow of the market can also be explained by the birthrate cycle and the number of peak spenders present in the economy. No matter what the exact explanation, the odds strongly suggest that we now face a twenty-year cycle of low expected returns. This will wreak havoc with all of our saving assumptions over the next twenty years. In the 691 observations we have for real twenty-year overlapping returns between 1947 and 2004, 98 percent of all returns following strong twenty-year returns were between 0 and 5 percent per year. Pretending these odds don't matter and will not affect our investment results over the next twenty years is a foolish and potentially very costly assumption.

The Boomer Demographic Descends

To all of this, add the sobering fact that for the first time in history, 78 million Americans are approaching the traditional retirement age of sixty-five. If the government is unwilling or unable to offer solutions, this huge cohort of Americans will be like a tsunami crashing upon our fiscal shores. By 2018, Social Security payroll taxes will no longer cover payouts, and the government will be forced to begin drawing on the Social Security Trust Fund's surplus. Worse, Medicare and Medicaid face looming shortfalls—Medicare alone will be saddled with deficits seven times larger than Social Security. According to the June 1, 2005, *Budget and Tax News* published by the Heartland Institute, the combined deficits of Social Security and Medicare will soar through the 2025–2030 period. According to the report, "Without changes in worker payroll tax rates or senior citizen benefits, the shortfall in Social Security and Medicare revenues compared to promised benefits will top more than $2 trillion in 2030 . . . [T]hese estimates, which come from the latest Social Security Trustees report, do not include the growing burden of senior health care costs under Medicaid." Note that these are nominal numbers, but even after inflation, they still top $1 trillion in *real* dollars. Finally, the report notes, "It shows that combined Social Security and Medicare deficits will equal more than 28 percent of federal income taxes by 2020. Roughly, this means that in just 15 years, if the federal government is to keep its promises to seniors, it will have to stop doing more than one-fourth of everything it does today. Alternatively, it will have to raise income taxes by one-fourth or borrow an equivalent sum of money."

The stock market is coming off one of the highest relative PE ratio and lowest relative dividend yield environments in fifty years. Seventy-eight million baby boomers are marching inexorably toward retirement and the Social Security, Medicare, and Medicaid promises that our government will have a difficult time honoring. Marry this to two hundred years of mean reversion, and the picture becomes difficult to ignore. This doesn't mean that we should hide all of our money under the mattress. On the contrary, the evidence shows us that certain types of equities will likely be among the best performing asset classes over the next twenty years, but we must be very particular about what we invest in.

I believe that these conditions also reinforce the ascendancy of those asset classes for which we have the highest forecasts, that is, higher dividend yield stocks. When baby boomers realize that they must be more responsible for their own retirement incomes, it is easy to see them flocking to higher dividend stocks as a way to improve their portfolios' returns. Investor demand pushes prices higher, which would make the forecasted returns for large-cap value stocks with higher dividend yields consistent with our forecasts. But the story is not enough—without the long-term data showing the cyclic nature of twenty-year returns, these too would be nothing but stories. But married to the data, they begin to explain why the market might indeed favor small-cap stocks and large stocks with high dividend yields in the coming two decades.

What Might Go Wrong

While our twenty-year forecast is well supported by historical fact and current valuation and demographic conditions, I can almost guarantee that at some point over the next twenty years it will appear to be *exactly* wrong. Time and again, history has shown how willing investors are to completely ignore the facts in the face of short-term emotions and stories. It may be a brand-new technology or industry or the reemergence of an existing industry, but it will happen again. When it does, large-cap growth stocks will soar in the short term, perhaps to the detriment of small-cap stocks and large-cap value names. The press, no doubt, will issue breathless stories about why it is "different this time," and why the current hot companies are not subject to the same laws of economics that have asserted themselves throughout history. And since we humans habitually overweight the short term, it will be extremely tempting to use that short-term performance to dismiss the longer-term forecasts presented in this book.

Sadly, this behavior is also consistent with our long-term forecasts, which *require* that investors' irrationality will continue to persist. If it didn't, something fundamental about human nature would have to change. If people stopped behaving irrationally, if hope stopped trumping experience, if emotion and fact sat equal on the scale, markets would cease their mean-reverting ways and become rational. In purely rational markets, fads would disappear and investors would price securities consistent with their true value, relegating irrational exuberance, outsized despondence—and twenty-year cycles—to the dustbin of history. Lucky for us, the chances of that happening any time soon are remote.

The Markets of Tomorrow

It could turn out that the next twenty years will be the first and only time that markets fail to revert to their mean. There is an *infinitesimal* chance that large-cap growth stocks could outperform small-cap and large-cap value stocks. But the odds of that happening are decidedly small. Even if it were to transpire, how bad could our recommended allocation do versus other investing options?

One of the great things about my recommended allocations is that they offer exposure to all styles and capitalization categories. The majority of the allocation is to large-cap value names, which typically have higher dividend yields and lower risks. Even if large-growth stocks go on to dominate, we'd *still* have a portfolio allocation favored by the odds and supported by all of the historical fundamental facts that suggest that paying the moon for a security leads to poor performance. And because we are explicitly rejecting the idea that you can time styles and markets, we will also have an allocation to whatever style or capitalization happens to be performing well.

Blink and It's 2026

Another very human characteristic is that time seems to move more quickly as we age. My son will be twenty-one when this book is published, but his first steps don't seem that long ago. The same is true for his younger sisters, who are now lovely young women, not the babies I so vividly remember. Time will pass differently for all of us, but the future will be here for us all sooner than we can imagine. What that future will be is up to us *today*.

Throwing our hands in the air and deciding that the future is unknowable may sound like an easy way out. But I am quite sure that sticking with the status quo and leaving your portfolio invested in large-cap core and growth stocks will leave you profoundly disappointed twenty years from now. Doing nothing *is* making a choice; it's just a bad one. Fanciful thinking will not make our futures happy and secure, nor will it ameliorate the hopes for what you will have to provide for your retirement. It may ease your anxieties today, but it will profoundly increase your anxieties to-morrow. Unless you save and invest your money today, being very careful as to what types of stocks and bonds you invest in, your investment future may be perilous.

If you decide to put the advice from this book into practice, you will at least be putting the odds on your side in what is sure to be a challenging market environment. Remember to rebalance your portfolio at least annually, ignore the day-to-day movements in the market, and keep your eye on the long-term ball. If you can do that, you'll be well ahead of the majority who failed to act. Act now, and the markets of tomorrow might be able to fulfill your dreams.

Index

advice:
  from author's books, 228
  one crucial piece of, 235
  online research and brokers, 227–28
  online specialty brokerages, 229–30
  outsourcing your anxiety via, 233–35
  problems in, 230–31
  Value Line software, 228–29
  value of, 231–32
  what to look for in an advisor,
    232–33
Allais, Maurice, 132
all-cap value strategy with growth twist,
  171–74
aluminum stocks (1950s mania), 11,
  32–33
Amazon.com, 89–91
American Depository Receipts (ADRs),
  153
American Express, 149
America Online (AOL), 36, 91–92, 95
AMEX, and the Dow, 138
Applied Micro Circuits, 8, 13
"Are Investors Reluctant to Realize
  Their Losses?" (Odean), 119
Arnold, Daniel, 136–37
asset allocation, 69, 73–74, 201–24
  annual contributions, 215, 220
  assumptions about, 202–4
  big differences in, 222–23
  bonds, 220–21
  conservative, 206–8
  conventional, 204–6
  equities, 204
  flexible, 210
  in 401(k)s, 196
  other, 221–22
  preferred, 208–10
  real estate in, 221–22
  rebalancing, 215
  stock selection strategies in, 211–12
  twenty-year forecast, 213–15

automobile manufacturers, 94–95
availability error, 120–21
Avon, 34

baby boomers:
  "generation Jones," 139–40
  as investors, 138–40
  retirement of, 139, 143, 247–48
  twenty-year phases of baby busts and,
    140
Bank Bradesco S.A., 94
Barclays Global Fund Advisors, 181,
  184, 186
Barker, J. M., 9
behavioral finance, 13, 14
  and availability error, 120–21
  biological causes of, 131
  and bipolarity, 133
  and fear of regret, 119–20
  and halo effect, 121–23
  and hindsight bias, 129
  and mental anchoring, 127–28
  and myopic loss aversion, 123–27
  and narrow framing, 123–27
  and overconfidence, 128–29
  and prospect theory, 117–18
  and representativeness, 129–31
  and risk, 117–18
  and twenty-year money cycle, 131–32
Behavioral Finance (Montier), 116
Behavioral Trading (Dorsey), 132
Benartzi, Shlomo, 123
Bezos, Jeff, 120
bonds:
  asset allocation, 220–21
  correlation of stocks and, 107
  and default risk, 100, 113
  in ETFs, 186
  and 401(k)s, 195–96
  and interest rates, 101, 107, 109,
    111–12
  intermediate-term, 100, 107–9, 113–14